Advance Praise

"On the TV show CHiPs, I played California Highway Patrol Officer Poncherello, a Latino hero. I can tell you right now that my friend Tony Arismendi is the real deal! He is an awesome, compassionate, spiritual, and courageous human being who conquered innumerable challenges and became an incredible FBI agent."

—ERIK ESTRADA, actor, producer, police officer, and humanitarian

"Tony Arismendi has lived the American Dream and is an inspiration for all. He survived the dangers of Venezuela as a child and leveraged the lessons learned to succeed in life and his career. Our friendship was forged under the microscope of the FBI Academy, where you truly see what a person is made of. Tony's tenacious work ethic, strategic thinking, and intelligence enabled him to become a great FBI agent and survive some of the most dangerous undercover assignments that resemble a Hollywood action movie. His many exploits leave you on the edge of your seat, cheering for the good guys."

—MICHAEL E. ANDERSON, FBI Assistant Special Agent in Charge, Retired

"As an FBI Supervisory Special Agent back in the late 1990s in San Diego, California, Tony Arismendi often wore open-collared silk shirts, gold chains, and pleated pants to work. He looked and sounded like he was right out of Miami Vice. When it came to investigating and catching some of the biggest drug traffickers in the world, Tony felt nothing was ever too big, too far away, or too difficult to accomplish. He understood how to think like a crook and invent outlandish undercover scenarios so that the criminal targets never suspected they were dealing with the FBI. Tony is unbelievably charismatic, funny, and loyal. Those are the very same qualities that made him an outstanding FBI agent."

—KEITH A. BYERS, FBI Assistant Special Agent in Charge and Legal Attaché, Bogotá, Colombia, Retired

"Tony Arismendi is not just a friend; he is like a brother to me. We met in the trenches while working with the FBI and DEA in a joint task force targeting organized crime, drugs, and gang organizations. We formed a unique partnership and took down some of the most dangerous and heinous criminals in Los Angeles. An incredibly talented FBI agent and great leader, Tony served with honor and courage. I'm proud to have worked with him and to call him my friend."

—RALPH ORNELAS, Commander, Los Angeles Sheriff's Department, Retired

"I first met Tony Arismendi at the FBI Academy. My job was to train, mentor, and supervise him along with forty-seven other new agent trainees. As a walking example of the harsh realities of government service, as a US Marine and later as an FBI agent, I knew then and now what it takes to survive and thrive. I saw in Tony those qualities and more, the distinctive attributes that would later make him into an exceptional FBI agent."

—EDMUNDO MIRELES, FBI Supervisory Special Agent, Retired. Recipient of the FBI Medal of Valor for exceptional heroism

"Anthony "Tony" Arismendi is a man I have grown to know well, as manifest in numerous capacities and dimensions. He is indisputably an authentic Renaissance man, yet one who brought his own American refinement to the Old World mantle, which itself is deeply rooted in his rich heritage. Professionally, his acute intellect and kinetic creativity seemed to always dazzle the good guys and doom the bad ones. Many can innovate and others implement, and some deliver while others inspire; Tony dynamically mastered all these traits, as attested throughout his storied and intriguing FBI career. His book greatly reflects his character, which I believe is his greatest strength, and certainly composes the man I would follow, regardless of mission or destination. Suffice to say, his book will take you to places and experiences and sensations many have never known, and more so, fewer have ever lived."

—EDWARD L. FOLLIS, Associate Special Agent in Charge, DEA, Retired. Author of *The Dark Art: My Undercover Life in Narco-Terrorism*

"When I first met Anthony (Tony) Arismendi, I thought he was a Buddhist monk driving a BMW. Little did I know that this guy was one of the most badass FBI agents around, taking down some of the most dangerous criminals in the world at that time. I only came to learn that after we had known each other for some years, as we enjoyed discussing our shared interests in Eastern philosophies, Buddhism, and spirituality. Now I know why he never sits with his back facing the front door."

—**GEORGE MEEKER**, film, television, and commercial producer in Los Angeles

Outsider Agent

Outsider Agent

THE EXTRAORDINARY ADVENTURES OF
AN IMMIGRANT AND MYSTIC IN THE FBI

Anthony Arismendi
WITH LARRY CANO

HOUNDSTOOTH PRESS

COPYRIGHT © 2022 ANTHONY ARISMENDI

All rights reserved.

OUTSIDER AGENT
The Extraordinary Adventures of an Immigrant and Mystic in the FBI

ISBN	978-1-5445-2704-8	*Hardcover*
	978-1-5445-2702-4	*Paperback*
	978-1-5445-2703-1	*Ebook*
	978-1-5445-2701-7	*Audiobook*

Contents

Advance Praise	i
Author's Note	xv
1. Scottsdale Bank Robbery	1
2. Caracas	27
3. Colegio	37
4. Wax On, Wax Off	47
5. Awakenings	57
6. Inspiration	71
7. Separation	77
8. The Home of the Brave	87
9. Salt Lake City	93
10. "Are You Gonna Finish Those Fries?"	107

11. The Friendly City	115
12. College	127
13. Newlyweds	141
14. Looking to the Stars for Guidance	147
15. Becoming a Father	151
16. Las Vegas	153
17. Undercover Boss	163
18. When Opportunity Meets Preparation	169
19. Quantico	175
20. Special Agent Ed Mireles and the Miami Firefight	181
21. Sixteen Weeks	189
22. Transition	205
23. Breach	217
24. Debrief	227
25. Home	233
Epilogue	245
Appendix I: Juan Bautista Arismendi	253
Appendix II: Luisa Cáceres de Arismendi	263
Acknowledgments	269
About the Author	273

To all the outsiders.

It is not the critic who counts; not the man who points out how the strong man stumbles, or where the doer of deeds could have done them better. The credit belongs to the man who is actually in the arena, whose face is marred by dust and sweat and blood; who strives valiantly; who errs, who comes short again and again, because there is no effort without error and shortcoming; but who does actually strive to do the deeds; who knows great enthusiasms, the great devotions; who spends himself in a worthy cause; who at the best knows in the end the triumph of high achievement, and who at the worst, if he fails, at least fails while daring greatly, so that his place shall never be with those cold and timid souls who neither know victory nor defeat.

—**THEODORE ROOSEVELT**, excerpt from the "Citizenship in a Republic" speech delivered by the former president on April 23, 1910, at the Sorbonne, Paris, France

Author's Note

OUTSIDER AGENT IS BASED UPON MY LIFE STORY AND IS AN ATTEMPT to accurately recreate events, locales, and conversations from friends, coworkers, family members, and my memories of them. Additional details were obtained from diaries, letters, family videos, and open sources, including newspaper articles and televised news reports. In some instances, specific characters and timelines have been changed to maintain the continuity of the narrative and for dramatic purposes. The names of selected individuals, places, identifying characteristics, and details have been changed to preserve their anonymity and privacy. If there are any mistakes, inaccuracies, or oversights, they were unintentional and I take responsibility.

This book has been reviewed by the Federal Bureau of Investigation (FBI) and was approved for publication. In the approval letter, the FBI stated, "We concluded none of the information presented falls within a restricted area of disclosure. There is no objection to the publication of your work, as presented." The opinions and views expressed in this book are mine and do not represent the opinions and views of the FBI.

CHAPTER 1

Scottsdale Bank Robbery

It was the summer of 1991, and a relentless, white-hot desert sun threatened to melt the dull, black pavement of a downtown street in Scottsdale, Arizona. On this Friday afternoon in June, ripples of heat rose off the asphalt in blinding waves in front of a local bank. An all-too-typical scorcher, but one that even the most hard-boiled inhabitants complained about, wondering how the planet could get so hot and why human beings would choose to subject themselves to these hideous 120-degree temperatures.

An entire city block was cordoned off by lines of police officers, who struggled to keep curious gawkers and zealous reporters at bay. It seemed the whole town had gathered to witness a bank robbery gone wrong, with armed assailants holed up inside. There were reports that at least one hostage had been shot and lay bleeding on the polished floor of the Valley National Bank at the corner of Scottsdale Road and Oak Street.

A robber had entered the bank at 2:30 p.m. dressed in fatigues, leather gloves, and boots, with camouflage netting over his face. Displaying a shotgun, pistol, and grenade, he calmly notified those present that he was robbing the bank. At the outset, he held eighteen customers and bank employees hostage but sporadically released some of them throughout the standoff. Released hostages later commented on how he apologized to them for the inconvenience he was causing while he simultaneously duct-taped a shotgun to the back of a woman's neck, assuring himself that the barrel would remain pointed at her head. He then promised to blow her away if anyone tried to stop him and informed the terrified hostages that he was infected with HIV.

Outside, television news teams fought for the best angles, reporting on how the local police were outgunned by the robbers, who supposedly had high caliber weapons. One reporter also mentioned that the Scottsdale Police Department did not have a SWAT team and, thus, had called in the FBI and its special tactical unit.

A speeding convoy of beige, gray, and white American-made sedans rolled up, and a team of FBI agents sprang into action. With military precision, the men began preparations without much discussion. From one car, Special Agent Anthony Arismendi stepped out, popped open his trunk, and began pulling out and sorting his combat gear. Anthony, who went by Tony, was twenty-nine years old, lean, fit, and maintained a stoic countenance and bearing of an ancient warrior, making him appear much older.

A senior agent and team leader, Chris Brennan, rushed past barking orders.

"What do we have?" Tony called out, having been summoned via pager and only given an emergency code and address.

"Hostage situation is all I know," responded Brennan, a highly experienced combat veteran and tactical operator with the elite FBI Hostage

Rescue Team. "I'll have details for you in a minute," he added. "We're goin' in before those crazy bastards shoot somebody."

"Roger that," Tony replied.

He rapidly studied the men assembling and discerned that most were either new to the Bureau, or were second-stringers. The seasoned SWAT operators were unavailable, leaving that task to the FNGs—Fucking New Guys. Tony surmised the veteran agents were either in court, working undercover, or out of town on other assignments. Dozens of lives rested in these rookie agents' hands, some of whom lacked the experience of having been there and done that. Tony counted eight fellow agents marshaled to the scene and realized they would be at half strength numerically as well. He wasn't quite sure of the situation but instinctively knew the more agents, the better the odds, and having twice that number on his team would have been ideal. He also acknowledged that he was excited as hell for this opportunity.

Tony followed a prescribed and familiar ritual of meticulously layering on the necessary accessories of a modern-day warrior that he stored in his trunk. He put on a fire-retardant shirt, pants, and gloves, a Kevlar vest and body armor, and Hi-Tec boots. Over everything went an outer mesh vest with numerous pockets for carrying an array of smaller items he might need. He grabbed the leather wallet that held his badge and credentials, and placed it in one of his front pockets. The vest also held wires to his earbuds and a throat mic that rested against his vocal cords. The mic was designed to pick up the slightest vibration, allowing him to speak in a whisper and still be heard by his teammates.

Finally, he strapped on a field belt laden with ammo clips and other tactical gear, including a cumbersome brick-sized radio transmitter he affixed to a belt at the small of his back. His pager remained in its position on his belt, set to vibrate only. When he finished, only his head was left uncovered.

The heat was getting worse, if that were possible, and he began to sweat profusely under the weight and thickness of his kit. Tony threw a couple of salt and electrolyte tablets into a bottle of water and chugged it, knowing he might well be in position for a long time in the searing heat, thoroughly dressed and sweating heavily. It might be a while before moving out—part of the "hurry up and wait" game that threatened to drive everyone crazy. Tony's training included always being mindful of his level of hydration. He knew that being adequately hydrated is key to maintaining one's mental edge—and vitally important when heading into a potential firefight.

Tony grabbed an MP-5 submachine gun from a gun rack built into the roof over the front seat of his car. He unholstered his Sig Sauer P226 semi-automatic pistol from his side and did a quick weapons check on each gun, making sure they were locked and loaded and that the suppressor on the MP-5 was good and tight. He checked his homemade grip on his Sig that he had fashioned from a piece of a bicycle inner tube he cut and stretched over the pistol's handle. He had tightly wrapped small strands of rubber on top of the tube, making a comfortable but efficient custom grip that wouldn't slip out of his hand, even under the hot and sticky conditions he now found himself in. It was one of many tricks of the trade Tony had picked up and assimilated into his repertoire.

He threaded his arm through the sling of the MP-5, allowing the thirty-one-inch gun to hang freely off his chest. Tony was a big fan of that weapon. He liked its compact size, light weight, and maneuverability. It fired a 9-millimeter round that held sufficient knockdown power yet did not deliver a tremendous recoil, which greatly enhanced the gun's accuracy. It was for that same reason he carried a 9-millimeter Sig Sauer sidearm as well. His handgun fired with a smoothness he preferred. He was confident that the exceptional Swiss/German technology of this weapon was superior to any other pistol he had ever fired. With the 9-millimeter, he was willing to give up some stopping power for accuracy, a trade-off many shooters are willing to make. The MP-5 boasted a thirty-round capacity, and on fully automatic, he could empty the clip in a just a few seconds. Even so, he preferred keeping it on a three-burst setting for each trigger pull. He reasoned that it saved ammunition, and he would rather not have to drop a clip and reload in the middle of a firefight when fractions of a second could be the difference between life and death. And he had a gnawing feeling that this time, each second was going to matter.

As he leaned over to grab his Kevlar helmet, Tony reached into a front pocket of his vest and pulled out a laminated photo of his wife, Alyssa, and his young son, Anthony, that he kept inside of it. He took a moment to study it. There was his firstborn, an American, smiling brightly at him through the photo as he clutched his favorite stuffed animal, a little oversized mouse little Anthony named "Spuds Mackenzie." And here was Tony now, living out his life's dream and feeling privileged, he thought, to find himself in a position to protect and serve the people of the great country that had taken him in and made him one of their own.

Tony brought the photo to his lips and kissed it, sending his son and his wife a silent blessing, hoping they could feel it too. If he didn't come out of this alive, Tony prayed that Anthony would always know that he loved him more than life itself. Closing his eyes, Tony asked God to see him through this and, if he should fail to walk through his front door later that evening, to look after his family.

He carefully placed the picture back into his pocket, fit a pair of Bollé goggles around his helmet, and pulled a black Nomex balaclava slowly over his head. He strapped his helmet on snugly, gripped the MP-5, and headed resolutely toward an uncertain fate, knowing all hell was about to break loose. A hostage rescue was a scenario for which he and his team had prepared through hours of disciplined exercises. But controlled training was one thing—the real deal was quite another. Tony was all too aware of the myriad things that could go wrong, sending events spiraling out of control in a millisecond. A hostage rescue requires precision above all else. With innocent victims to think about, they couldn't charge in with guns blazing. They would have to work like brain surgeons and perform a delicate procedure.

Tony entered the staging area and tried to wipe away the sweat flowing into his eyes. Squinting, he saw his team assembled beneath the only reprieve from the scorching sun, a solitary cottonwood tree whose leaves stood motionless on this eerily still afternoon. He saw the figures of his fellow agents in the foreground melt away, blending into the waves of heat that danced off objects in the background, distorting his entire field of vision into a blistering, undulating blur.

Brennan knelt on the scorching asphalt, reviewing blueprints of the bank spread out on the ground along with a veteran agent, Riley Martin, and the rest of the surrounding squad. Riley was a legend in the Bureau, an incredible agent who had seen and done everything. His specialties were bank robbery and violent crime, and fellow agents looked up to him for his many accomplishments. Riley was a few weeks from retirement and looking forward to it, ready to hang up his shield and ride off into the sunset. He had recently bought a motor home that he and his wife planned to meander around the country in until they got good and tired of traveling or ran out of gas. Riley was the anchor, the second in command, and was about to lead this bunch of B-teamers through a locked and possibly barricaded door and into an impossible situation. It was unspoken, but everyone, including Tony, was secretly relying on Riley to see them through.

Tony approached the huddle, and Brennan waved him in. The bank's head of security stood among them, hunched over the plans, and sweat from his downturned face rhythmically dripped onto the paper. He reviewed the floor plan, pointing out the only two entrances to the bank building, one in the front and another in the back. The man explained that the bank was intentionally constructed to thwart any attempt to break in—a mini Fort Knox. The roof was made of steel and reinforced concrete, so there was no easy way to get through. And neither the main glass entry doors on the bank's north side nor the teller's window on the building's south side were an option since both were made of three-inch-thick bullet-resistant tempered glass. Brennan pointed to a back doorway on the plan that was the only possible way in, a steel security door on the wall next to the teller's window.

Brennan considered the situation a long while, took a deep breath, and said, "Well, I've got some good news and some bad news, men." He paused again, studied the building plans, and added, "Hell, I'm afraid there isn't any good news."

Brennan then filled in the details. A getaway driver was seen outside of the bank but had since driven off. They were given a description of the vehicle, and there was an all-points bulletin out for it. The gunman inside had released several of the hostages, but the victims were rattled and gave imprecise information when interviewed. However, one man gave a bit of good intelligence. Because this man had military experience, they decided they would rely on his observations. The former hostage believed there were two gunmen inside dressed in camouflage, with perhaps a third accomplice waiting in a car outside. He offered a fairly detailed description of one of the robbers as well. The man had also counted about seventeen hostages.

The released hostage was a blessing, giving the team the kind of information a civilian may never have had the presence of mind to study and remember. But the most sobering news came when he confirmed that the gunman was amply equipped with high-powered weapons and body armor, and also had live grenades. The team first learned from the released hostage that the gunman told the hostages that he was suffering from AIDS and was prepared to die. It was early in the epidemic, and the full effect that the disease had on human life was still not yet known. Everyone was aware that people were dying from it in massive numbers. The fact that this gunman felt he had nothing to live for made the situation even more dangerous. The agents also knew enough about AIDS to realize they needed to protect themselves from blood and fluids that could surely be scattered all over the place once the shit hit the fan. The former hostage's observations got Tony's full attention, but he oddly found himself relieved at the same time. At least now they had a better idea of what they were up against.

Brennan let it slip that this was the worst hostage rescue situation he had ever been involved in. He quickly caught himself, realizing his mistake, and added that despite the complicated circumstances, he had full confidence in them. It was not going to be an easy rescue to execute, he said. Still, he was confident they could succeed if they relied on their training, discipline, abilities, and most importantly, upon one another.

SWAT Team Phoenix—Tony's in the back row, fourth from the left.

Right before a deployment.

The blueprints began to curl up under the intense heat, their blue lines rippled on the blaze of oversized, parched white paper as Brennan reviewed tactics one more time. The security officer produced a key and said it fit the single lock they would find on the back door. Brennan flipped the key to Tony, who stuffed it into a zippered pocket in his vest.

"Tony's breacher," the team leader shouted, and assigned everyone else a number from two to eight. Thoughts of the possible problems he could face in getting the door open and what he might face once he breached the door raced through Tony's mind. Brennan reminded the team that he would be in charge from the command post and that during the operation, Riley, #3 in the line, would be in charge on the ground.

Brennan said, "We've got the green light from Washington to do whatever we gotta do. Make your way to the bad guys, and if it's necessary,

Scottsdale Bank Robbery | 9

don't hesitate. Take 'em out. Okay?" The team leader paused to take a deep breath. His eyes misted as he said, "I love you guys. I love you all." He looked into his men's eyes through their goggles. He fixed on each one for a long moment. "You guys are my guys; you know that? You are my guys!" Brennan took another pause, then with a cracking voice, "Okay, let's do this!"

The men stood there a moment, taken aback. They knew Brennan had experienced every kind of scenario imaginable. He had seen combat and survived countless successful missions as a member of elite FBI hostage rescue teams. None of the men had ever seen him emotional. If a hardened vet like Brennan was worried, the men knew they were in for a world of shit. Tony also began considering the obvious.

Tony said, "Can I ask you a question?"

"Sure."

"You said they have grenades?"

"Yes, Tony."

"What if when we open the door, it's wired with explosives, or they toss 'em at us?"

Brennan paused a moment, took a deep breath, and answered, "Well, Tony, then a lot of people are going to die today."

Jesus Christ! Tony thought. At once, his mind started racing. What would his family do without him? Did he have enough life insurance to provide for his little boy?

Images began to flood his mind: his beautiful son hugging his mouse, their comfortable home in a nice neighborhood, his wife, his dog, and his family and friends. He mustered all of his willpower to force such thoughts out of his mind. He needed to stop thinking about his civilian life and focus on what he was about to do. He knew all too well that people depended on him as point to lead the way, and he wasn't about to let them down.

Riley, now in command, made sure everyone was correctly positioned, then directed the agents to quickly work their way to the bank's windowless side wall.

"Shit!" Tony muttered out loud. He would be the first guy in, and if he pushed that door open to a live grenade…Then he caught #4 staring at him, and each knew what the other was thinking. Brennan's words were still ringing in their ears too. Tony's teammate had a little boy about the same age as Anthony. He and his wife had just had twin girls. Tony took another moment and glanced from agent to agent, knowing this was probably the last time he was going to see some of these guys alive or vice versa.

The beeper clipped to his belt vibrated, and he expediently silenced it. It was Alyssa.

* * *

She was calling, wanting Tony to call her back. She was wondering where he was and why he was late again. Tony had promised to take them to the mall and dinner, and she was growing impatient. Of course, it didn't help that Alyssa was eight months pregnant with their second son, whom they had decided to name Dillon. Now more than ever, she looked forward to a break from chasing their high-energy toddler around the house all day. Sitting at home, Alyssa began to slowly boil. Although resigned to the sacrifices the family made for Tony's job, she would openly admit to her close friends and family that she was beginning to resent the effect the Bureau had on their lives.

Alyssa initially went along with Tony's long-time yearning to become an FBI agent and even encouraged him. Before he accepted his appointment to the FBI Academy, she and Tony had spoken about the struggles they could expect for countless hours. To prepare for her life as the wife of an FBI agent, she met with other wives and even read books on the topic. But the dissonance between theory and practice, imagination and reality, was beginning to rear its head. She was trying though. She knew that a substantial percentage of marriages involving law enforcement officers did not last, and she was determined not to find herself on the wrong side of that statistic. She loved Tony and admired his resolve and determination. She respected his decision to become an FBI agent, even as she fought her resentment that he had left a promising job as the youngest assistant store manager of a major department store chain in the history of the company. His virtually guaranteed seat in the executive suite would have ensured their family's financial success. Within a few years, Tony would have risen up the department store ranks, and she would be raising their family in a fashionable neighborhood with Tony commuting to a place like Manhattan in a Beamer instead of driving to a field office in a government-issued Buick in Phoenix. More important to her, Tony could have begun to show Alyssa's wealthy and self-made father that she made the right choice in a mate.

In their home in Ahwatukee, a stylish housing development in South Phoenix, little Anthony sat on the living room floor, petting Ninja, the family's Rottweiler, while he watched *Sesame Street* on TV. He laughed giddily at the Cookie Monster, his favorite character, merrily singing "C Is For Cookie." Ninja, a stout female Tony had trained personally as a guard dog, was a member of the family and Anthony's best friend. Short of being able to recite poetry and read Aristotle, the animal was more human than dog.

Alyssa, Anthony, Ninja and Ranger.

On the afternoon of the Valley National Bank robbery, Ninja sprang to life and bounded to the entryway when she heard a banging on the front door. Ninja's training was such that she did not bark to offer a warning. Instead, she sat waiting to pounce should the visitor be a foe and not friend. Alyssa answered the door to find two neighbors who eagerly asked if she had been watching the news.

"What news? What happened?" Alyssa asked in a panicked voice. She urgently switched channels and found live coverage of the bank robbery hostage situation on almost every channel. She settled on one and focused her eyes on a line of FBI agents at the ready near the bank's rear door.

"Daddy!" Anthony screamed as he got up from the floor, ran over to the set, and put his finger squarely on the screen. "That's my daddy!" he gleefully exclaimed. He quickly picked his father out of the line of agents and put his finger accurately planted on Tony's helmet.

Alyssa turned away from the set, her jaw dropped, and the color drained from her face.

※ ※ ※

The agents were melting under the oppressive heat, held in by their layers of clothing and gear. Most people could not have stood up to these conditions. But the youth of Tony's team and extensive training in the Arizona heat worked in their favor. To become agents, the members of the team were put through a rigorous selection process. Most had advanced college degrees, were lawyers, forensic accountants, or technical wizards. Others possessed a shopping list of achievements as fighter pilots or had served in the military as Special Operations personnel. The members of the FBI's SWAT team endured even further selection and testing. Being a member of the team demanded an even higher level of commitment due to the extra time training took and the unpredictable hours. To be prepared for anything they might encounter, many members of the team ran marathons and triathlons and were exceedingly well conditioned.

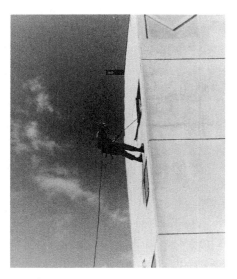

FBI SWAT training exercise

FBI SWAT training exercise

FBI SWAT training exercise

Tony was only one of two people in the squad who were not former military. He felt a definite pressure to push himself in hopes of earning the respect of those who would have his back when the chips were down. But Tony was someone who had always thrown himself entirely into any new commitment. Where the SWAT training called for a particular exercise once or twice, Tony would perform the task five to ten times. On one occasion, he struggled to perform a task that required him to use his dominant but broken hand. Rather than sit it out, he forced himself to complete the task repeatedly with his weaker hand—again and again until he had mastered it. He recalled the tenacity of his FBI class counselor Ed Mireles, who had carried on and finished a gunfight despite losing the use of his arm. If Ed could do it, then Tony could train through an injury.

While at Quantico, Tony trained the Marine way. A portion of the expansive Marine Corps base at Quantico, Virginia, was provided to the Bureau by the US Marine Corps. In 1934, the Marine Corps allowed the FBI to use its gun ranges for training, primarily due to an incident the year before. While three police officers and one FBI agent were escorting Pretty Boy Floyd through a Missouri train station in 1933, criminals looking to free Floyd opened fire on the group, killing the three officers and the agent. Following a public outcry, FBI agents were given the authority to make arrests and carry weapons for the first time. By 1972, the FBI had built a full training campus at Quantico, forever linking the Bureau and the Marine Corps. Not only did they share a base, but many of the agents were former Marine Corps enlisted soldiers and officers, some of whom became instructors at the FBI Academy. As such, the Bureau adopted the Marine way of physical training and marksmanship. Sit-ups, pull-ups, and push-ups with a whole lot of running were the mainstay of their PT (physical training), and they worked on it daily. Huge muscles and bulkiness were discouraged in favor of lean and mean. Physical training also included lessons in boxing, wrestling, and defensive tactics consisting of a variety of martial arts movements intended to disable an opponent. These activities required speed and cardiovascular conditioning. Maximum endurance and quickness were what was sought after. The motto for Tony's academy class was "Leaner! Faster! Stronger!"

FBI SWAT training exercise

The team rushed across the parking lot and made their way to the east wall of the building, still in plain view of the crowd outside the bank and the news cameras. The media were following their gospel—"If it bleeds, it leads"—and this story had huge potential in that department. News choppers circled overhead with a persistent *thwack, thwack, thwack*—their din so loud it nearly drowned out the squad's voices in their earpieces.

The team glided in stealthily, shielding their advance from the bank's front, and crept in unison to the windowless side wall, staying low and using scant ornamental shrubs as concealment. By cutting all power, the bank's security officer managed to disable the video cameras that would have given anyone at the monitors inside a view of all four sides of the bank. Unfortunately, this also plunged the space into darkness and dramatically increased the temperature inside as the air conditioner powered down.

Each agent knew precisely what their individual assignments would be once they entered the bank. They had perfected their drill over time. It was well choreographed and synchronized and, if executed correctly, would ensure the best odds for success. The agents knew that in battle, the advantage goes to an entrenched enemy, and the gunman couldn't be any more embedded than he was holed up in that bank.

The initial entry itself was all up to Tony as #1—the breacher. Once he opened the door, Agent #2, positioned next in line behind Tony, would heave in a flash-bang grenade, creating a huge distraction. Made up of an explosive charge with a mixture of magnesium and potassium chlorate, it would create a flash equivalent to 300,000 candlepower and a bang exceeding 160 decibels. The flash-bang would have the desired effect of disorienting everyone in the bank but would pose no danger to the hostages since there would not be any actual shrapnel, which would buy the team precious seconds to seize command of the situation from the gunman. Following its detonation, Agent #2 would be the first in the door, covering the left arc, with Tony swiftly following, covering the center arc. The next agent would go in and move to the right. They would continue the pattern until everyone was inside. They would keep moving, each covering their section of the arc, fighting their way in until they eliminated the threat and secured the bank. The discipline to remain focused only on one's area of responsibility is mastered through repetitive training and a great deal of faith and bonding with other members of the team.

In his peripheral vision, Tony saw crowds of people. He quickly studied the reporters, onlookers, and a news van. *Shit, bullets are going to fly*, he thought. *Why the hell don't the police get these people out of the way?* The agents stood with their backs to the media. Still, Tony could see the team was in plain view of the TV cameras, whose photographers took cover behind a four-foot wall, their tripods and cameras with their long lenses extended like periscopes on a submarine.

At the ready and awaiting the final order to proceed to the back door, Tony felt thousands of eyes boring down upon them as the agents held their position. Tony was sure the onlookers saw them as some kind of action heroes imbued with superhuman abilities with those three bold letters, FBI, stenciled on their backs. All that remained was for Tony's team to come in and save the day. The good guys were about to get the bad guys and mete out justice in a real-life portrayal of the classic western *The Magnificent Seven*, in which Yul Brynner recruits a band of gunslingers to protect the town from bandits. Tony realized this is what folks had come to expect from the FBI.

The FBI had recently continued to have a string of high-profile successes, including the counterespionage case that broke up the John Walker spy ring, the arrest of the killer of Judge Robert Vance in Alabama, and the arrest of infamous mobster John Gotti in 1990. Most similar to the present situation, a shoot-out in Miami in 1986 that saw the good guys take out two real-life bandits, but at a high cost.

Tony glanced over his shoulder at the growing crowd and thought, *Hey, everybody, we're human just like you. We bleed. We put on our pants one leg at a time. We want to come home to our families tonight, just like you do.*

Images of his boy flooded his mind again. He envisioned Anthony later in life, watching the videotapes he had recorded so Anthony would have some idea who his father was if Tony did not survive an operation such as the one in front of him now. There was footage of Tony assuring Anthony that he was wanted and loved and that his dad had died doing something he loved and felt was his duty. He shared a lot of the kind of insight and encouragement Tony received throughout the years from his father and grandfather. Tony could imagine Anthony saying years from now, "Yeah, here's my dad on video. He died in a bank robbery shoot-out when I was still in diapers."

Tony caught himself again, not allowing himself to dwell long upon such thoughts. He had a job to do, and this is what he signed up for. There were innocent people inside who had lives of their own and families waiting for them as well. They deserved the best that Tony and his team had to offer. Tony thought of John 15:13, a verse his father particularly loved. It spoke of a concept that had propelled Tony into the ranks of the FBI in the first place: "Greater love hath no man than this, that a man lay down his life for his friends." Tony resolved to "flip the switch" and put all of his conscious attention into the task at hand.

Since he was a child growing up on the streets of Caracas, Venezuela, where he had to fight for his survival repeatedly, Tony mastered the ability to "flip the switch" during a fight. He learned how to fix his attention so acutely that he could filter out anything and everything, including sights and sounds that had nothing to do with the situation at hand. He enjoyed the adrenaline rush, which instead of making him jittery, had the opposite effect of calming him and allowed him to focus with laser-sharp clarity. Also, after years of martial arts training and meditation, he often found that time seemed to occur in slow motion, giving him a distinct advantage.

Tony was always amazed when he heard that little voice that came from somewhere deep within his psyche and gave him direction. Perhaps it was intuition, he thought, maybe some gift. Or maybe his guardian angel. In any case, he always listened to that voice and obeyed. It had never let him down and would save his life many times in future operations. In fact, during another operation, as his team made its way down a hallway of a home, that little voice told him to move to his right. He had intuitively listened, not questioning where the insight or direction originated. Shots rang out, and bullets passed by his left, striking another member of the team farther back in the line.

He glanced back at his team, locked in place behind him, and saw Riley, the designated entry team leader, starting to shake. They were standing there, everyone in position with their weapons ready to go, and now every head was turned, staring at their rock, watching him crumble before their eyes.

His shaking continued. It was the all-too-real fight, flight, or freeze response, and now Riley was in the grips of the third and least desirable reaction when he blurted out, "Okay, okay, you know what? Okay, Tony, you're not #1 anymore, now you're #2." Turning to another agent, "And you, you go #1. And uh…"

At that, Agent #2 stepped up, his face right in Riley's, cutting him off. "What the fuck? What are you doing? You can't change the lineup now! You'll fuck up everything. You can't change anything now!"

But Riley started to go over the new lineup again, still trembling, eyes glassy, now speaking as if he were having a nice chat with himself.

During an FBI SWAT operation.

Agent #2 got into the man's face again, but he looked right through him and continued muttering. The rest of the team stood motionless, frozen in a state of disbelief and fear.

Tony slipped his hand firmly between the two men and said, "Goddammit, what the fuck are you two doing?! We don't have much time before we all DIE here. Goddammit! STOP FIGHTING! There are people inside that we have to get out! We don't have time for this shit!"

They were witnessing an all-out meltdown. Riley was plummeting, envisioning his imminent death, while the rest of the team was trying to keep it together. It was evident that he would be of no use to them now. No one could fault him—he broke down, that's all. Who could lay blame on a guy who always fought the good fight in a protracted war against society's worst? Some of the men must have been thinking, *Here is one of the most experienced guys around, who has been on missions to hell and back so many times. He's seen everything, and now he knows this is it! Fuck!*

Agent #2 took over. "Places," he whispered into his mic. "Line up."

And the agents tightened their line.

Riley moved himself toward the back of the line.

The team kept in close contact and awaited the command to get into its final position for the assault. An incident that occurred in Sacramento in early April had a significant influence on their tactics now. A four-person team armed with 9-millimeter pistols and a shotgun had taken forty hostages at an appliance store. While negotiations took place, a Sacramento Police Department SWAT team snuck its way through the ceiling from a nearby store into a rear storage room hidden from the gunman. A two-person sniper team stationed at the front had orders to shoot any gunmen on sight. When one hostage was sent outside the front door to retrieve a bulletproof vest dropped earlier in a failed exchange for a hostage, one of the snipers opened fire at the gunmen. At that instant, the glass door slammed shut. The bullet was deflected by the thick plate glass and missed its target. The gunman who had been the intended target began shooting the hostages. At the sound of the gunshots and breaking glass, the SWAT team hidden in the rear rushed forward and caught the gunmen by surprise, killing three and wounding one, but not before three hostages were killed and nine wounded. Tony's team had recently done a series of field exercises because of that tragic event to glean a better working knowledge of what different calibers and loads will do when various rounds are fired at different kinds of targets. A .308 round, the traditional choice for FBI snipers, can easily pass through a cinder block wall. But a shot through tempered glass will unpredictably deflect the trajectory of the bullet, even an armor-piercing round.

The two snipers on Tony's team positioned themselves in a hiding place atop the hellishly hot tar roof of a tire store across the street, about 130 yards away. Ethan was a veteran of the sniper squad, while Sam was a former accountant, new to the FBI, and fresh out of sniper school on his first assignment. They had their tripod-mounted sniper rifles, both Remington M24s, positioned next to one another. They focused their aim on the front of the bank building, the sights of their weapons fixed upon the glass front entry doors of the bank. These were the same doors through which the gunman previously released hostages and the most likely point that they might get a shot. The snipers had to take turns on their scopes—the scorching heat limited their time to effectively aim before needing a break. They prepared for any chance at a clean shot, should the suspect dare to open that front door. They knew they couldn't risk shooting through the glass itself.

At his command center, now an outfitted motor home, Brennan called for a radio check and final weapons check and issued a few more tactical orders. Through their earpieces, Brennan told them that negotiations had broken down. The gunman had made all kinds of ridiculous demands, including a helicopter ride to the airport while he kept three hostages and money. The gunman gave a 5:00 p.m. deadline for the demands to be met. Based on several factors, FBI command concluded that the gunman was not going to let himself be taken alive. When the gunman had walked into the bank and taken everyone hostage, he immediately directed an employee to alert the police. Also, he had waited well into the standoff to demand any money, which made it seem like ransom was an afterthought. With this information, it was clear to the FBI that there was not going to be a peaceful surrender. This scenario had all the ingredients of an inevitable gun battle and worse: the possibility that the hostages would be killed. The FBI's seasoned negotiators had done their best, but at this point, there was nothing more they could do. It would now be up to Tony and his team to save the people inside. The clock was ticking.

Brennan said, "Alright, let's do this!"

Tony whispered into his mic, "God, Luck, and Training!" Their mantra, and they needed to hear it now more than ever. Tony repeated the phrase silently to himself a few times. He was ready.

Everyone was in position, the agents were in line, ready to move, and the snipers were at the ready as they lay cooking on top of that tire store, somehow holding it together in their rooftop inferno.

"Move!" Agent #2 hissed into his mic.

The squad sprinted in unison toward the corner of the building, rounding it and finally arriving at the south side wall. Tony maneuvered under a protruding teller's window and thought he saw the outline of a gunman trying to spot them. Thankful he was able to avoid detection by staying low under the cutout of the box window, he signaled for the rest of the team to join him and keep their tight formation.

Tony crept up to the security door, still hoping they would not be seen under the teller's window. He stopped next to the door, and each man began locking his knee behind the knee of the man in front of them. Once they were physically connected this way, they put their hands on the shoulder of the man in front of them. When Tony was ready, he could tap the agent behind him, and that signal would be repeated down the line and sent back up. Once it returned to Tony, he would be good to go. Once Tony moved, the rest could clearly feel the tactile command and move as one.

Tony got his key out and inspected the door. "Jesus Christ!" he hissed involuntarily. He stared incredulously at the heavy steel door. There were two locks, not one, as he had been told. Tony's mind raced. Would one key fit both locks? The men watched him intently, wondering why Tony had frozen in his tracks. They had no difficulty hearing him when he murmured, "Fuck!"

Tony got back to the business of finding a way through that metal door. Surveying the locks, he raised the key and tried to fit it into the top lock. He inserted it steadily and twisted. It didn't turn. *Okay, maybe it fits the other lock,* he thought, and he would have to try to pick the first one.

"God *dammit*! What the *fuck*?" Tony mumbled to himself. Glancing at his watch, he realized there were only a few precious minutes before the robber's deadline. He had to get this right.

Time stood still, as if present, past, and future locked into this one moment. Tony began to experience everything in slow motion. He glanced over his shoulder at #2 behind him and saw his eyes fixed on him, unwavering. The others down the line wore the same expression: watching, waiting, poised to spring into action. With a calm and intense focus, he took a couple of curved and jagged tools from his utility vest pockets. Tony had some basic knowledge and training on the construction and operation of locks and how to pick them, but he was no expert. He was now all too aware that everyone was waiting on him. Perspiration poured in tiny rivers, soaking his clothes but doing nothing to cool his overheated, armor-clad body.

Straining to see inside the tumbler, he manipulated a pick, feeling for the pins, and set each one. Hoping he had found the right positioning, he listened for a faint clicking sound. He took the end of a tension wrench and cautiously tried turning the cylinders inside the lock. Was he turning the lock in the right direction? Having to guess, he tried turning the cylinder clockwise. Then *plink*! And nothing happened. The first lock did not open. Tony's heart dropped into his stomach.

He could hardly believe what was happening. He reached for the key again, held it between his thumb and index finger, and tried once again to insert it into the first lock, but by now, rivers of sweat completely obscured his vision. He wiped his eyes with the back of his sleeve and refocused his sight. Holding the key, he studied the lock, took a deep breath, and prayed that he could unlock the door in time for them to save the hostages inside.

CHAPTER 2

Caracas

FIVE-YEAR-OLD TONY SAT IN THE PASSENGER SEAT OF A SHINY NEW yellow 1967 Volkswagen Beetle, with his father, Eduardo Jesus Arismendi, at the wheel. His older brother, Eduardo, affectionately called Eduardito, sat in the back as they motored through the Fuerte Tiuna, a crowded cultural district of Caracas, Venezuela. Caracas, Tony's hometown and Venezuela's capital, was founded in 1567, forged in the crucible of Latin America's turbulent past. Subjugation and violence were the hallmarks of over two centuries of Spanish conquest and rule. The venerable city had since become a sprawling, overcrowded, and polluted metropolis with a population of three million. Throughout the years, its inhabitants had invaded every sliver of land in the Caracas Valley they could claim from the lush jungles that engulf the hills and mountainsides surrounding the city. Mount Avila, the tallest peak, stands guard between the city and the Caribbean, nine miles away. In earlier days, the mountains had kept the city safe from marauding pirates and always served as a fortress from invading armies during Latin America's tumultuous revolutionary times in its protracted struggle for independence. Caracas now has the unenviable distinction of being the city with the highest crime rate in the world, with more murders per capita than any other place on the planet.

A saving grace, however, is its year-round tropical climate where temperatures average a hospitable seventy-five degrees Fahrenheit, varying little from day to night and season to season. Jungles, with their wide variety of flora and fauna that cover nearly two-thirds of the country and their close proximity to Caracas, provide a bounty of lush and delightful scents that waft into the city on ever-present breezes, especially after one of the tropical rainstorms that regularly sweep across the land.

Venezuela's jungles are one of the most biodiverse places on Earth, a habitat for an abundance of colorful and venomous spiders, insects, and animals, along with an assortment of poisonous plants. Most spiders and insects are much larger in Venezuela and the jungles of South America than almost any place else on Earth. A Goliath tarantula that roams many of Venezuela's rainforests can reach sizes of a foot across with one-inch fangs. Bullet ants abound, so named because their sting can feel like being shot and is thought to be the most painful sting of any insect.

And there are aggressive wasps, like the tarantula hawk, that are up to two inches in length with a sting so powerful it can trigger a fatal anaphylactic reaction in people. And there are a countless variety of venomous snakes, some of which can kill a person in a matter of minutes.

Tony and his sister, Angela, both Ring Bearers at Aunt's wedding

Tony and his brother and younger sisters learned early about the types of lifeforms they lived amongst and which to avoid at all costs, a survival skill they had to master to stay alive. The Brazilian wandering spider, the most venomous in the world, can grow to six inches. Tony and his siblings became all too familiar with other creatures like it. While on a family vacation, one of the massive spiders made its way into the beach cottage where the family was staying. Recognizing the type of spider and the danger everyone was in, Mr. Arismendi Sr. soothingly told everyone to stay still while he picked up a broom, careful not to startle the creature. In one quick motion, he hurled the broom handle end first, spearing the thick part of the spider's body and killing it instantly. The heroics of Mr. Arismendi served as a reminder of the dangers that slithered and crawled throughout Venezuela.

The yellow VW made its way through hectic traffic and caught the eyes of people on the street and in other cars. The car was Tony's dad's pride and joy that he kept in immaculate condition; its buffed paint job and polished chrome glistened in the bright afternoon sunlight. Eduardo had his window down, a pleasant wind washing over his face as he took in the sights and sounds of the city and admired the towering and artful architecture of the government buildings.

Tony's father, twenty-nine at the time, was a strikingly handsome man with jet-black hair and a trimmed beard. More interested in philosophy than the insurance business he was in, he was a learned and kindly man who, earlier in his life, wanted to become a Catholic priest. He had enrolled in seminary but left before becoming a priest. He was educated in America and had mastered English. Later in life, he became an ordained Anglican priest. On this day, he was a proud father filled with anticipation of introducing his youngest son to his great-great-great-grandfather's memorial in a place called Paseo de Los Próceres—Walkway of the Founders. The monument is a national shrine to Simón Bolívar, the liberator of Latin America, and to ten generals and others under them who fought to secure independence for Venezuela and the other countries that would eventually evolve into modern-day South America.

Paseo de Los Próceres—Walkway of the Founders. Monument and national shrine to the leaders of the South American revolution and liberators of Latin America.

Monument to the Leaders of the South American revolution.

Tony was not accustomed to riding in a car. Before long, he got car sick and threw up all over the pristine vinyl upholstery. Eduardito, a year older than Tony, didn't waste any time teasing him about it and received a prompt rebuke from their father. Mr. Arismendi pulled over and cleaned up the mess without complaint, careful not to make Tony feel any worse than he already did.

They made their way to an expansive outdoor mall and parked in a sizable lot for tourists and visitors. They strolled toward the heroes' walkway, where two massive, five-story white obelisks jutted into a crystalline, azure sky. Tony glanced toward the jungle-clad mountainsides that ringed the Caracas Valley. His attention was drawn to the many birds circling the skies or darting in and out of the trees, shrubbery, and other vegetation that flourished around the site. He studied them with rapt attention and listened keenly to their squawking, calling, and chirping. He was fascinated by their vibrant colors, their variety, and their sizes and playfulness. With over 1,400 bird species in his country, his father was quick to point out a new one whenever they spotted a bird they had never seen before. One of his favorite activities he did with his dad at home was to put out wild bird seed and watch the birds feed. They were his friends, and he delighted in watching them swoop and dive down.

The trio found their way down the avenue toward the monument, which was built on both sides of the walkway and consisted of two rows of giant dark bronze statues perched atop twenty-foot-tall black marble pedestals that faced one another and ran the length of the memorial. Behind the pedestals and facing one another rose the two building-sized bleached marble walls adorned with bas-relief carvings on their front sides that depicted key battles in the series of wars for independence that took place in the early nineteenth century. Names of the many generals, officers, and other heroes of the struggle for liberty from Spain were inscribed and listed by rank. In the middle, on the right side of the entryway and elevated above all others on a higher platform atop the pedestal, stood the largest statue—a dark bronze image of Simón Bolívar, rising some sixty feet off the ground, his left hand on his sword and his right arm extended in a gesture of peace. The sculpture of his likeness was prominently centered in front of the towering white wall, with BOLÍVAR inscribed in oversized gold raised lettering on the pedestal beneath his figure. His countenance was that of a confident leader, the great emancipator who had won the good fight and was now inviting his people to follow him.

Simón Bolívar, *El Libertador* (The Liberator), was the leader of the South American revolution and first president of the Gran Colombia, the name of the first and short-lived republic liberated from Spain in 1819 that included Colombia, Panama, Ecuador, and Venezuela. It was Bolívar's master plan and great dream to unify South America into states, as the revolutionaries to the north had just been successful in doing in their lands. The Gran Colombia would later splinter into the separate countries known today, and Bolívar would go on to become the first president of Bolivia and one of the early presidents of Peru.

Next to the statue of Bolívar resided the twenty-five-foot-tall statues of four of his generals, two on each side, each atop the pedestal but standing beneath the distinguished leader. All of their names were displayed in bold relief on the black marble pedestal beneath each statue. On the other side of the walkway was a twin display with a matching black marble pedestal and six statues the same size and proportion of the others that faced them. On that side of the memorial were the likenesses of six other esteemed generals immortalized in bronze. Directly facing Bolívar stood the statue of General Juan Bautista Arismendi, Bolívar's chief of staff and second-in-command. In a relief carving on the white marble obelisk behind him was a dramatic depiction of the Battle of Pichincha in 1822 that led to the liberation of Ecuador.

They reached the General Arismendi statue, and Tony's father prepared for a speech. Eduardito had heard it before, and his attention drifted. All this was new to Tony, who took the sights in through his child's eyes.

Mr. Arismendi knew that Tony, and even Eduardito, for that matter, were too young to grasp the full meaning and importance of what he was about to say, but that did not stop him from continuing. His father and his father before him had been sure to impart the family's history to them, and Tony's father was not about to fail to live up to tradition. He directed the kids' attention to the three-dimensional image of their great-great-great-grandfather standing before them, set against the dramatic carvings on the relief behind him with the ARISMENDI family name boldly inscribed in stone beneath the imposing figure. The famous general stood erect and proud, both hands clasped on the hilt of his long-sword, his gaze permanently fixed upon them, and his magnificent cloak cascading to the ground.

General Juan Bautista Arismendi memorial, at the Paseo de Los Próceres—Walkway of the Founders.

After taking a long and dramatic pause, Tony's father proudly exclaimed, "There, my boys, is your great-great-great-grandfather. He was Simón Bolívar's right-hand man and one of the founding fathers of our country and, therefore, of all Latin America. I want you boys to always be proud of your heritage. The same blood that ran through his veins is running through yours."

At that, Tony peered down at his arms as though to see his blood coursing through his body.

After another long moment, Mr. Arismendi turned to Tony and asked, "Well, Antonio, what do you think of your great-great-great-grandfather?"

"He sure was big!" was Tony's reply.

Tony's father chuckled. "No, mijito, this is only a statue of him. Like a picture, only better," he said. "He was a man—like me—and like the man you will become. Like your great-great-great-grandfather, always be willing to fight for what is right and just."

It was these and other stories that Tony was told as a boy at family gatherings and in the classroom about the heroism of General Arismendi that provided a wellspring of inspiration at times that he faced his own challenges. He was also told stories of the heroics of his great-great-great-grandmother, Luisa Cáceres de Arismendi, that inspired awe in him as well.

CHAPTER 3

Colegio

TONY HAD GROWN INTO A WIRY EIGHT-YEAR-OLD AND WAS SEATED in a classroom at Santo Thomas de Villa Nueva, a Catholic school. The school was referred to as "el Colegio" by Tony and his classmates, and it might as well have been a college for all the advanced studies the students were exposed to. The curriculum included Latin, chemistry, physics, world history, literature, and advanced calculus—all required before students were allowed to graduate from high school. Tony wore the mandatory outfit: shorts the kids called "pantalones pio-pio" with a starched white shirt and knee-high socks. Long pants were reserved for boys fifteen years and older. The priests, many who came from Spain and Italy, were of the Salesian order. The teaching, supervision, and discipline were strict. Failure was met with a liberal dose of corporal punishment. The priests wore traditional long black robes with a belt that hung down one side. This belt was at times used to crack down on a child passing a note, messing around, or losing focus. Another favorite way the priests got your attention was by pinching the offender's earlobe very hard and dragging the student away to be hit with the belt or a ruler. Tony periodically found himself on the receiving end of the Salesian discipline system.

It was the start of a new school day, and both his teacher—a nun—and his fellow students were subdued. One of the desks sat empty. Tony's teacher asked her students to pray for the child who usually would have sat at the vacant desk. The child had been taken by kidnappers and was being held for ransom, an all-too-frequent occurrence amongst Tony's peers. The nun prayed that the kidnappers would return the young man to the safety of his family, but the students knew better. Kids who were abducted were often killed even after their families paid a ransom. Or they were maimed or blinded and set out on the street in another city somewhere and given a begging cup, never to be seen by their families again. Newspapers did not censor the brutal images of such events, publishing them for all to see. More than once, a horrified Tony saw the desecrated body of a friend or classmate on the evening news or prominently plastered on the front page of the newspaper. These were the harsh realities Tony was forced to reconcile with at an early age—realities that contrasted greatly with his social standing and background, and the spiritual foundation his kind-hearted father took considerable care to instill in him.

Hearing or reading about such things made him sad and, at the same time, angry. He wondered how God could allow these kinds of brutal acts to happen to good people. At his young age, he questioned a deeper meaning of life. He longed to grow up quickly so he could get his education, grow fit and strong, and begin to do something about it.

When he contemplated his future, Tony was invariably drawn to the military or the police. Always mindful of his family's military tradition and his relatives on both sides of the family that served in leadership positions in Venezuela, he was certain he'd follow in their footsteps. A great uncle on his mother's side was then the Minister of Defense. One Arismendi was a former minister of foreign affairs. Several others were generals, doctors, and diplomats. When he was a boy, one of his uncles worked in the Ministry of the Interior and brought ten-year-old Tony along on a three-day expedition into the Amazon. The group met with an indigenous tribe native to the area and learned about the use of blow darts dipped in frog toxins to kill their enemies. They chopped through the jungle with machetes and crossed rivers. Tony remembered with fondness his Indiana Jones–style outfit he wore on that trip.

On another occasion, he accompanied his father on a work-related excursion into the jungle. Along the way, they took a ferry across a shallow river. While crossing, he saw a cattle rancher beginning to coax his herd across the water. Unbeknownst to Tony, the river teemed with deadly flesh-eating piranhas. Tony watched in amazement as the man sliced the side of one of the lead cows and pushed it into the current to distract the schooling fish. The water churned and boiled, and in a few short minutes of frenzy, a full-grown cow was reduced to a mere skeleton as the fishes' razor-sharp teeth did their work. On horseback, the rancher quickly drove the rest of the herd safely across.

During a family excursion.

This disturbing image stayed with Tony as yet another reminder that growing up in Venezuela meant he had to be on his toes at all times in order to survive, as unseen dangers were present everywhere. The ability to operate on high alert and be aware of danger long before anyone else was what later kept him alive in numerous incidents in his years as an FBI agent.

Tony's surname was widely known in Venezuela. His classmates were also a constant reminder of his background. To them, he was "Arismendi," and kids and teachers alike referred to him by his surname. "Hey, Arismendi, do you want to go play fútbol?" a friend might ask. Or "Arismendi, seven meters squared equals how many millimeters squared?" a teacher might inquire. All the kids were aware of which families were which. When Latin American history was taught, General Juan Bautista Arismendi's name might well be brought up in the same breath as General Santiago Mariño's or General Antonio Páez's, and the descendants of those great leaders might be sitting in the classroom alongside Tony.

The principles of standing up for justice, becoming a leader, and helping others were embedded in Tony's genetic makeup. His exposure to universal spiritual principles, carefully orchestrated by his father, collided with often gruesome life experiences. All of this bolstered his growing desire to serve and protect others, an aspiration that was becoming fixed in his young psyche.

One time after class ended for the day, Tony made his way toward the schoolyard gate, looking for Eduardito. He saw his brother talking to a couple of other kids on a corner just off the school grounds and began walking toward them. Out of nowhere, a gang of rowdy street kids appeared and blocked Tony's path. Eduardito saw this and sprinted toward Tony while the kids he was talking with quickly ran away. Eduardito, ever Tony's protector and a boy who loved to brawl, reached his brother's side and stood shoulder to shoulder with him as the gang edged closer, backing the two brothers up. One kid demanded their money. Another came close and tried to grab Tony's books from under his arm.

Thinking the two light-skinned brothers were immigrants, their leader taunted, "Why don't you two go back where you came from? Get out of our country."

"This is our country," Tony yelled back.

The kid took a swing at him and caught him right on the side of his face, knocking Tony backward. The kid came at Tony again, but Tony dropped his head down and smashed it into the kid's nose, running right through him and dropping him to the ground in a heap. Tony sprinted off, with Eduardito fast on his heels. They ran like crazy, zigzagging through the streets with the gang chasing after them, closing in fast and shouting threats.

Tony and his brother made it to a stash of rocks they had hidden under a stoop of a house along their route home. They flung them at the approaching kids and drove them back until they ran out of ammunition. The brothers then dashed away again with the gang still in hot pursuit. They came to the base of a tree, scattered some leaves, and retrieved two hefty sticks they'd wrapped with tape at each end for a better grip. The kids came upon them, and they stood side by side and swung wildly, occasionally making contact with the gang members, who bobbed and weaved. The brothers tried desperately to get their licks in, eventually managing to drive their pursuers back. Suddenly one of the gang members pulled out a switchblade and waved it wildly while another reached into his pocket and pulled out an ice pick. Tony and his brother hurled their sticks at their tormentors and again sprinted away, running for their lives.

Tony was fast, faster than his older brother. One of their pastimes was to pretend they were being kidnapped, call out an escape route, and make themselves disappear at lightning speed. Tony could see in his mind's eye a path up the drainpipe of a two-story building, where he could execute some moves as though he were Spider-Man. He could scale the roof, jump down the other side, and sprint to the next block in a matter of minutes, always beating Eduardito in a race. The boys needed all of their skills now. They knew it was on, and they were in a primal fight for survival.

Racing down their street and almost home, they looked back and saw the gang almost upon them and closing fast. Nearly all the kids had knives out now, and they meant business. Eduardito reached another hiding place, pulled out a box that had been cleverly concealed, grabbed a loaded .38 caliber revolver, and pointed it at the biggest kid. Tony got behind his brother, and the big kid put his hands up and backed away with the others glancing around, not knowing if they should stay or run away.

Just then, a federal police car pulled up, and the gang scattered, with its members scurrying in different directions. Eduardito put the gun down and rattled off to the police as rapidly as he could what had just happened. As he explained, both boys unbuttoned their school shirts and revealed an undershirt with a distinctive insignia. The school uniform and the T-shirts alerted the officers that not only were they friendlies but that both boys were from a prominent family. Eduardito explained that he and Tony were Arismendi and Pardi. In Venezuela, the local police would just as soon shoot someone than ask questions, so it was vital for kids like Tony and his brother to let the police know what family they were from. One of the policemen picked up the weapon, unloaded it, and both officers escorted the brothers the rest of the way home.

The two police officers, with the sheepish Arismendi brothers, huddled in the parlor of a classic two-story old Spanish villa where the Arismendi family lived with Antonio and Angela Pardi, Tony's maternal grandparents, along with a small domestic staff. The stately home was originally built in the early 1900s and had been in the family since, proudly displaying the Pardi family's coat of arms over the front entryway. It occupied an acre in a well-to-do section of town that provided relative safety for the boys, at least until they left their block.

Tony wore a ruby-red and rapidly rising bruise on his face as he prepared to take his medicine in front of his elders. The police officers showed deference toward the adults, particularly Tony's grandfather, who hovered close by with a concerned eye on his grandchildren. Tony's father couldn't believe the boys had taken his gun and stashed it out on the street. The boys' mother, Cecilia—a spry, strong-willed, and attractive woman of twenty-eight—was angrier that Tony let himself get hit than anything else. If Tony was fearful of being kidnapped or beaten up by a gang of boys, he was even more afraid of facing his mother if he were to fail to stand up for himself or lose a fight.

"How could you let someone walk up to you and hit you in the face?" she accused in her staccato Spanish. "Someone picks on you—you put them down. You win, and that's it. Don't come home crying to me."

"Mama, Tony did great," Eduardito offered. "He headbutted the one that hit him and knocked him down. But there were too many of 'em. And they had knives."

Tony's mother felt better now as she suppressed a satisfied grin. The two officers exchanged a knowing glance. They were all too familiar with strong Latin women. Tony's father thanked them for escorting the boys home and saw them out.

If Tony's father was the pacifist monk of the family, his mother was the warrior. She was from a family of Italian descent from a mountainous region on the border of Venezuela and Colombia. Tony's grandparents, Antonio and Angela Pardi, were from a prominent family that rivaled the stature of the Arismendis. His mother's family, from hearty stock and with their roughhewn ways, preferred settling matters with the sword or, in modern times, with the barrel of a gun. Their idea of negotiation was to shoot it out.

One time, Tony was hanging out with Eduardito and a group of Eduardito's friends. A local man felt the group had taunted him and confronted the kids, looking to teach them a lesson by pummeling the one he thought had mouthed off. Tony, the youngest and smallest at the time, moved behind the group of kids toward the steps of his grandfather Pardi's home where he lived. Tony's grandfather must have heard the commotion from inside the house, as he appeared out of nowhere, racking the slide on a rifle to chamber a round, and pointed the gun directly at the grown man threatening the kids. His grandfather told the man to "get the fuck away from these kids" or he would kill him. Wisely, the man backed away and never bothered them again. To Tony, it was no wonder his mother was so tough, with parents like that.

Their family lore had it that they were descendants of the Countess di Ragusa. The countess, from Sicily, fell deeply in love with a commoner who was a military officer. Forbidden to marry her, he swept her away and emigrated to a small village in the mountains of what was to become Venezuela. The couple lived modestly alongside the villagers and made a happy life for themselves. They had many children, including Cecilia Pardi's forbearers.

At his young age, Tony had already witnessed his mother in action. There was the time she got into an argument with a Russian lady over a parking place. The Russian took a swing at her, then quickly got back into her car and locked the doors. Cecilia promptly slashed all four tires so the woman could not go anywhere. Another time, Tony's mom was followed home from the bank by a robber on a motorcycle. She refused to relinquish her purse and paid for it with a broken hand, but managed to hold on to her money and eventually chased the robber off.

Tony and his siblings often found it entertaining as they hid behind the doorway, taking turns peering through a keyhole when their mother and father would fight like cats and dogs. They watched in a combination of delight and horror as their mother would fling a variety of projectiles against the walls with full force, their father leaping and diving like an NFL receiver to save the knickknacks, clocks, and vases from certain destruction. But later in life, Tony was forever grateful for her influence and headstrong determination. He and his brother would grow into the kind of individuals who could always handle themselves and stand up for themselves in any situation. It took years of practice, hard work, and determination, but the two brothers became masterful fighters in their own right.

CHAPTER 4

Wax On, Wax Off

MANY YEARS BEFORE THE POPULAR MOVIE *THE KARATE KID,* Tony and Eduardito met their own Mr. Miyagi in the form of Shoko Sato, a former international karate champion and master from Miyagi, Japan, who settled in Caracas. Tony and Eduardito sat in the waiting room of the sensei's dojo while their mother talked to the teacher and signed papers. Both boys were filled with skepticism, and Tony clearly did not want to be there.

"Look at that guy," he whispered to Eduardito. "He doesn't look like he could hurt a fly!"

"How's he supposed to teach us how to fight? I'll bet Mom could kick his ass," Eduardito replied.

The wiry and fit young man, not yet thirty, stood ramrod straight with a commanding presence and poise. He was immaculately dressed in a starched white karate gi, his red belt embroidered with gold Japanese characters that signified master level, the highest rank attainable in his system, and neatly tied in a proper knot. He wore a close-cropped eraser-head haircut, and his grooming was immaculate, down to his manicured nails.

Tony at Master Shoko Sato (kyoshi) Dojo in Caracas, Venezuela

The floor of his gym was made of high-quality sugi cypress that had been smoothed by countless hours of students kicking off of it or sliding and tumbling on it. Three walls were covered with bamboo planks, the fourth with full-length mirrors and a ballet bar. Makiwaras, which Tony would first hate then later learn to love, stood like sentinels along the walls. These were boards of different heights, some with padding, some without much, that students were encouraged to strike to toughen their hands.

When Tony's mom motioned the boys over to meet Shoko Sato, the first thing Tony noticed about the man were the large calluses on each of his knuckles. Before Tony's mom left, she told the boys to pay attention and work hard. They were both going to become karate experts if she had anything to say about it.

Tony's multiyear training began. At first, he didn't want to go to karate class after school and on Saturdays, and would try anything and everything to get out of it. But he learned that his protestations fell on deaf ears and soon reasoned that he was better off going to class and getting thrown around by his instructor than bearing his mother's wrath. She was not beyond taking a belt to him for this or other transgressions. Often, Tony would sport welts on his arms or wherever, with belt-hole marks painfully visible.

The martial arts training was not easy. Tony and his brother worked hard but made little progress at first. Their sensei was a taskmaster, while at the same time fair and consistent. The master took a particular interest in Tony, realizing that although he was thin and frail, he had great potential as a fighter. The master knew Tony had plenty of time to fill out, and he was quick and very athletic—attributes that can't be learned. In the fighting world, there is an old adage that speed kills, and it's true. In hand-to-hand combat, speed, timing, and accuracy can overcome size and power.

Tony would learn a new move or series of moves that always surprised and motivated him. He could do things he'd never been able to do before and always wondered how he had done them. Sometimes he could not believe that it was he who had actually performed what he had just pulled off. Before long, reacting to punches and kicks coming at him was automatic. Without thinking, he could respond to just about anything thrown at him, then deliver an offensive series of effective counter punches, kicks, leverage moves, and throws.

Tony, now twelve, and Eduardito, fourteen, both sporting buzz cuts like their teacher's in the era of long hair, watched their fellow competitors at a karate tournament in Caracas with uneasiness if not trepidation. They were both overwhelmed by the spectacle, the bright flags and banners everywhere and rock music blaring so loudly that they could feel the bass lines reverberate in the center of their chests.

They had to cover their ears as raucous supporters for a large contingent of fighters from the US clapped and cheered wildly. Their eyes were glued to them as the foreigners warmed up, unnerving them and making them feel thoroughly overwhelmed. The boys worked out in a modest dojo and had never seen such skill exhibited by contestants they were about to face. Some of the kids came from as far away as Europe, and most moved like Chuck Norris. Tony swallowed hard, fighting an impulse to get out of there as quickly as he could.

Tony with Master Shoko Sato (kyoshi) at Dojo in Caracas, Venezuela

Their instructor felt they were ready and had insisted they compete; despite that, they were both only wearing green belts and were pitted against opponents who wore black or brown around their waists. To Tony's surprise, the contest was full contact. The fighters wore neither footgear nor gloves and pulled no punches. The only protection allowed was a cup.

Tony turned to Eduardito and said, "I didn't know this was full contact! This is real fighting!"

Shoko Sato stood stoically behind the boys.

"And look at these guys, they're all black belts or brown belts. How are we supposed to beat them?" Eduardito asked.

At that, their sensei leaned in and said in his Japanese-accented Spanish, "What difference does a belt make? *No importa cinturón.* It's only color on a piece of cloth. Nothing to do with fighting. Only matters what's in here," he said as he tapped the side of his head with an index finger. "And in here," and thumped his chest with his other hand. "You want a black belt? Here. Here's a black belt!" And the master removed his leather belt from his trousers and handed it to Tony. "Now you go out there and fight. You go do your best. Rely on your training and your conditioning. You will see what happens then."

Their teacher closely studied Tony's fearful expression when Tony saw a fighter from another school warming up with impressive high kicks, spins, backhands, and reverse heel kicks. "Never mind that fancy stuff. Doesn't work in combat. Looks good for show, but no good. Stick to the basics," he said. "You win in here. You win on the street—with the basics. Basics never let you down."

Over the time of his training, Eduardito managed to incorporate elements of his strong suit into his fighting style. He preferred to run opponents down, then pin them against a corner or cut off angles on a mat. He was a relentless aggressor and impervious to pain. He was willing to absorb shot after shot to get his opportunity to take an adversary out, usually in a one-punch brawler style. Eduardito fought first, being in a heavier weight class than Tony, and managed a respectable third place.

Tony, who felt totally outclassed, was next to step onto the mat. He had been matched up against a smart brown belt who wore a colorful emblem of a rival school embroidered on the back of his gi. The kid had long black hair in a ponytail and was clearly the crowd favorite. Intimidated, Tony danced, bobbed, and weaved a lot in the first round. He was caught with a couple of well-placed strikes and kicks, but there was no serious damage. In the second and third rounds, he quickly found that he could rely on his technique and his exceptional reflexes. He was able to avoid getting hit and promptly counter to deliver strikes and kicks of his own with speed and accuracy. He won his first match.

Tony showcasing one of his trophies at Master Shoko Sato's (kyoshi) Dojo in Caracas, Venezuela

Tony's second fight was against a cocky black belt from the United States who, thankfully for Tony, was far more concerned with the way he looked than being effective on the mat. His opponent was bigger than Tony with muscles that belied his young age. Once the match started, Tony found he could keep moving, bouncing, jabbing, and confusing the boy.

"That's it, Tony. Stick and move. Stay active. You're faster than him!" Shoko Sato yelled.

Eduardito chimed in, "He's all show and no go! Tire him out!"

Tony did just that. He'd circle left, then move right. He'd feint a punch, then hit the kid with a spinning back kick. He scored with some good strikes and kicks and managed to finish the third round with a serious peppering of rat-a-tat punches that won him the fight on points and moved him to the championship fight for his weight class.

But he was hit with a dilemma when he stepped onto the mat to see that his final opponent was someone he had not conceived of preparing for—a girl. A referee signaled for the fight to start; spectators in the packed arena went crazy, cheering for her. At first, he scoffed at her, turning to his sensei and his brother with a look that asked, *What am I supposed to do now?*

The resolute brown belt charged in hard and introduced herself with a couple of hard shots that caught Tony squarely in his face. He refused to hit her until she got him down, jumped on him, and tried punching him a few times, landing a few as the round ended. In the ensuing rounds, he got his first real-life lesson that a girl can be a formidable opponent on the mat, and he was forced to fight all out. He had to use everything he had learned to keep her off him. Near the end of the final round, he managed to step in and grab the collar of her uniform as he shifted his hip into her, tossing her to the mat with a perfectly executed judo throw.

For a moment, she lay motionless. He was so proud of his work that he turned his back to his fallen opponent and raised his arms in triumph as the crowd roared.

Just as he caught his brother's eyes in the audience that pled with him to turn around, his self-congratulatory reverie was rudely interrupted as his opponent leaped to her feet, let out a thunderous and terrifying *"Kiai!"* as she hooked a quick right, then left to Tony's ribs. Tony felt the air leave his lungs, and before he could muster any kind of counter, she caught him with the knife-edge of her right foot on the back of his left knee, and he went down.

A horn sounded, and the fight was over, saving him from further embarrassment. The girl's last-second heroics won her the match.

Shoko Sato congratulated his student for his accomplishment afterward. For the first time, Tony saw a smile that replaced his usual reserved and dignified expression. The wise sensei emphasized three crucial aspects of fighting for the boys that day:

One, never prejudge your opponent. "You don't know what he—or in this case she—knows! You could be fighting someone who knows much more than you! Man or woman. Big or small, no matter. You fight everyone the same. And you always fight to win."

Two, never celebrate a victory or dwell on a defeat. "You do your best and use all of your training and your skill. The result will be what it will be. You can celebrate one day and cry the next. Stay neutral."

And three, "Never turn your back on your opponent!" he said, barely suppressing his amusement, while Eduardito laughed uproariously.

Later, when their master pulled up to the family home, Mrs. Arismendi quickly scurried out to meet them. With gleeful eyes, her satisfaction apparent, she watched her boys tumble out of their teacher's small car with two glistening trophies. Tony's, the bigger one for second place, was almost half as tall as he was.

Problems with the gang of street kids continued for both Eduardito and Tony for years, but it would soon come to a showdown. The gang members were mostly older boys now, in their midteens, as were Tony and his brother now too. Individuals would come and go, but the gang remained mostly intact, as did their overall disdain for the Arismendi—the brothers had to be on constant lookout. The gang had become hardened, and while some of them might appear like innocent kids, most of them could cut your heart out, hand it to you, and not blink.

What kept things in check was Mrs. Arismendi's vigilance in refusing to let the boys walk home, always picking them up from school in her Volkswagen Beetle. Tony and Eduardito were safe behind the school's high fences, and their mother made sure of it. But one day, Eduardito insulted the gang leader, yelling something at him through the fence. Respect meant everything—the hoodlum was forced to set an example. The gang blocked the path of their car at the first stop signal off the school grounds and thugs surrounded it. They demanded the brothers get out so they could be properly beaten up or worse.

Mrs. Arismendi jumped out in a fury and confronted them. "¿Quién es el jefe? Who is your leader?" she demanded to know. Her boldness threw them off, stopping them dead in their tracks. The boys stood there, speechless. Looking around, she quickly figured it out and turned to the kid. "You're such a badass. You need all of your friends to fight my son? Why don't you fight him one on one? What are you afraid of?" She opened the door of her VW and leaned into Tony. "You're going to fight this guy. And you'd better fucking kick his ass because if you don't, I'm gonna kick yours!" She turned to the gang members and said, "What do you have in your pockets? Show me." She made each kid empty their pockets and told them she was going to hold their weapons until after the fight.

Without his buddies or any weapons, the gang leader was no match for Tony. He played with the kid a while, deftly moving and bouncing while blocking the kid's best shots, or making him swing wildly into thin air. Tony would be right there in front of him, and then he wouldn't. He ended it by working his way inside and then feinting a high left strike to turn the guy's head, while simultaneously reaching around to the nape of the guy's neck and grabbing his long hair with his right hand. He swung his right foot behind him and pivoted, jerking the leader's head right into a light pole. He knocked the kid out cold.

Instead of the gang turning on Mrs. Arismendi, the gang members instantly became her new best friends. It was Señora this and Señora that. They patted her on the back. If she had harbored any aspirations of gang leadership, she could have quickly inherited a loyal band of her own right then and there.

Long after this incident, Tony would often reflect upon it in amazement, always wondering how his mother had managed to take control of the situation, disarm an entire street gang, and not get the three of them killed. Best of all, neither Tony nor his brother were ever bothered by the gang again.

CHAPTER 5

Awakenings

IN THE MARTIAL ARTS WORLD, THE CONCEPT OF *SIFU* OR *SHIFU* in Chinese, or *sensei* in Japanese, has emerged to represent a master or teacher. For the Chinese, more accurately "master-father." The fighting arts developed in China from ancient monasteries where monks practiced martial arts both as a way to achieve harmony of mind and body in their spiritual advancement, as well as a practical way to keep themselves safe as they traveled from village to village ministering to the populace.

The word *kung fu* (or *gongfu*) has its origin from Mandarin and translates to "working man." It can also mean "skill achieved through hard work." *Karate* in Japanese means "empty hand." Both forms had their roots in fighting systems passed down from a master to student and enabled commoners to defend themselves without weapons—or to be able to utilize everyday implements such as staffs, pitchforks, or hoes—and to be effective against attacking brigands or even against an emperor's army, if need be. In both regions, the rulers, at times, would accept the arts being taught, and at other times the study and teaching of the martial arts would be discouraged if not banned.

In the process, the concept of "master/teacher" would develop to make such a person a revered and vital member of society. A shifu might well have been a fully educated Shaolin monk who spent years in a monastery and was then sent out to live among the people in a particular village. A shifu's role might become that of a sheriff, judge, psychologist, teacher, doctor, general, and priest, all combined as one. He became the focal point of an entire community and was responsible for the health and safety of his people. He'd be the arbitrator in resolving disputes, a spiritual counselor, a healer administering remedies and setting bones, and importantly, a general preparing the villagers to defend themselves.

A shifu was a warrior-monk in charge of training his townspeople in the art of self-defense. Besides the obvious benefit of improving the collective ability of the village to defend itself against attacks, practitioners enjoyed the health benefits of the martial arts and all that went along with that: better blood circulation, improved flexibility, stamina, discipline, mental clarity, and focus. Long-term study and practice of the martial arts, many adherents claim, can lead an individual to experience spirituality in a new light. Through the dedicated practice of mental and physical discipline, new insights can be gained with regard to the perception of time, movement without thought, and the manipulation of *chi* or life-force energy. A learned master with the ability to disrupt the chi of an opponent is capable of victory by "short-circuiting" an adversary's electrical flow along meridians, it is claimed. All of these benefits, it is believed, can give an advanced practitioner a distinct advantage in combat for the protection of self and others while assisting in the continuing process of enlightenment of the spirit.

The concept of warrior-monk was certainly not exclusive to the Japanese or Chinese. The Knights Templar, Nagas monks in the Hindu tradition, and others throughout history upheld a similar principle. These were men who took vows of fidelity, chastity, and poverty and became experts at combat. They were, at the same time, servants of the cause of peace but, if need be, instantly became a deadly force against the powers of evil. They were allegiant to their rulers and to higher religious principles that gave them their motivation, if not their raison d'être. At first glance, it may seem a total contradiction that a human being could be dedicated to both opposing concepts of love and service on one hand and killing in the name of justice on the other. But in the tradition of the warrior-monk, there burned an implacable passion in them to serve God through the selflessness of service to others.

This concept is often symbolized in a traditional salute that is internalized in Asian martial arts that practitioners employ in different ways, depending upon the customs of individual martial arts systems. Most often, this is a variation of the right hand closed in a fist with the left hand open or covering the right. Then a bow, as a show of respect for the art and for the founders of the style, upon entering a dojo and upon leaving. Often, it's demonstrated before a teacher prior to receiving a lesson or for an opponent at the beginning and end of a sparring session or match. It's a sign of respect but also conveys a more profound meaning as a universal representation of the open hand of philosophy alongside the closed hand of war. The salute acknowledges the yin-yang duality of love/hate, peace/war, or health/destruction that exist simultaneously. Since the martial arts come from a self-defense tradition, they symbolize that opponents always have a choice to make. If one decides to fight, the practitioner, although preferring peace, is always ready to defend.

Tony's martial arts training and interest in the spiritual came about through his recognition of the presence of evil in the world and the need to overcome it, juxtaposed to his sincere desire to gain spiritual advancement. Like the warrior-monks of old, he was sure that to do God's work, one had to learn to confront evil and, once that goal was achieved, to dedicate oneself to protecting others.

Before the warrior phase of his training began with the venerable Shoko Sato, Tony had already experienced the transcendental component of the warrior-monk persona. When he was six, he and his family strolled down a busy downtown Caracas street on a typical balmy Saturday afternoon. Tony's parents were in the midst of yet another argument, while Eduardito's attention was focused on a soccer display in front of a sporting goods store that featured a life-size cutout of the Brazilian superstar Pelé scoring a goal.

A group of Hare Krishna devotees passed in the opposite direction, banging, chanting, and clamoring away. No one in the family paid any attention to them, except Tony, who was immediately and completely enthralled at the merry spectacle they created. Captivated as though by some mysterious force, he peeled off without thinking and blithely followed them. He was soon skipping and chanting with them. Tony found himself spellbound by the harmonious resonance of the chants, the incessant pounding of drums, and the enticing aroma of burning incense. It was a sensory overload for him.

He had no clue what was going on, yet he thoroughly enjoyed the totality of the experience. Everyone was so happy and kind to him. One man gave him a drum of his own. Another young woman dabbed a dot—or tilak, made from red sindoor powder—on his forehead over his third eye chakra, symbolizing the awakening of Tony's spiritual journey and ensuring his good fortune. Before long, Tony was singing and chanting along, oblivious to all else, including his parents.

When their bickering came to an end, his mom and dad suddenly realized he was missing. Tony's mom cried out in horror, "Where's Antonio?!" She turned to Eduardito, "Where'd he go? You were supposed to be watching him!"

In a panic, his parents, with Eduardito in tow, searched high and low for him for what seemed like hours.

About ready to give up and go to the police, Eduardito called out, "Mamá, look over there!" He spotted Tony across the street merrily marching along amid the band of devotees.

They were chanting their lungs out, with tambourines rattling, drums pounding, and cymbals crashing. *"Hare Krishna, hare Krishna, Krishna, Krishna, hare, hare!"* they sang out over and over to everyone on the crowded street.

Tony sang the loudest; he was having the time of his young life. He had a little drum fastened around his neck and was banging on it exuberantly with one hand while the other clutched a batch of sandalwood incense he handed out to any person who'd take one.

A few years later, Tony was preparing for the Catholic sacrament of First Holy Communion. He was devout in his faith and had aspirations of becoming an altar boy, a goal he accomplished a few years later. And like some of his relatives, Tony thought of perhaps becoming a Jesuit priest someday, as his father had pursued before meeting his mother, an achievement that would make any Latin American family proud. His father had explained that the Jesuits, Franciscans, and Salesians were highly intellectual, which drew him in. His mother's brother was also studying to become a priest.

Preparations in Catechism class began early. In Tony's school, First Holy Communion was a monumental event as a rite of passage and expression of faith, as it is in every Catholic school or family. Tony could hardly contain himself as the day approached. It would be a time of family celebration that he eagerly awaited. He was magnetically drawn toward intense inner feelings of agape love and a connection to God. These sensations were something so otherworldly and profound that he could not yet begin to define what he was experiencing.

Tony's first communion at eight years old

He would come to appreciate the mandatory daily chapel time and enjoyed the warm glow that overtook him when he prayed during the service. He had dutifully memorized each prayer and exactly when to say them. He excitedly awaited his First Confession, albeit with a bit of apprehension, and had prepared a list of sins he thought he should divulge to the priest when he had the chance. It was wonderful and mysterious, but knowing he would be forgiven and receive the body of Christ meant something to him. His classmates often complained when made to recite the Rosary, a set of prescribed prayers said in an order using prayer beads, but Tony grew to relish the ritual and practice. He felt connected and energized and close to God when he grasped the beads in his hand as he recited the proper prayer, then moved to the next bead and the next prayer.

One night, his mother left him in his room, kneeling at his bedside to recite his evening prayers. Tony began saying the Rosary, automatically letting prayer after prayer roll out of his consciousness. He repeated them over and over until they became a mantra—like he had learned to do with the Hare Krishnas. For what must have been hours, he knelt and fervently prayed until a dazzling display of lights filled his head, and a spectacular reverberating sound like the blaring of a trumpets began to fill his room and head. In an instant, he lost cognizance of where he was and eventually of himself.

He felt disconnected from his body, and a transcendental awareness swept over him; he was overcome by potent feelings of absolute knowledge, understanding, and clarity. And then he experienced a comprehension far beyond that of a typical boy his age. Intense feelings of joy and peace washed over him in waves followed by a quiet and penetrating sensation of oneness with everything.

At that moment, he was no longer a child; he had transcended beyond the physical world, entranced in a peak experience, an instantaneous epiphany of knowledge and understanding. He knew who he was and where he was headed in life. It was exhilarating and mystical, and gave him a taste of something he was not sure of and made little sense of, but resonated deeply in his soul. Of one thing, he was certain: whatever it was that he had experienced, he wanted more.

One time, Tony accompanied his father to visit friends at a Catholic monastery. His dad allowed Tony to play outside with some other kids who were also there while he visited inside. The kids had been playing a warrior game in a nearby field when Tony joined in. As he ran to join the kids, something on the ground caught his eye. The item had an odd shape and was strange-looking to Tony, who picked it up for closer inspection. Still unrecognizable. It turned out to be a shin guard abandoned by a catcher after a game of sandlot baseball, a game Tony had never played or had any experience with.

A strange sensation overcame him while he instinctively strapped it onto his lower leg. As he did, the thought flashed through his mind that he had strapped the strange item on many times before, as a warrior would in preparation for battle. Magically, the ground, trees, and walls of the abbey grew more vivid to his sight. The edges of the buildings nearby and his surroundings became crystal clear, and he saw himself as an adult dressing for battle, only he was strapping the guard onto a fully grown, muscular leg.

When his dad came out to check on him, he asked him, "What do you have there, Antonio?"

"I don't know what it's called, Papá, but I remember wearing it a long time ago," he answered.

"When was that?"

"When I was bigger," Tony said. "But they were made out of metal to stop swords."

His dad let that sink in and wondered how Tony had come up with that thought. He recognized that even though there was a small TV in his grandmother's room, it only had three channels, and Tony had never watched any of the old Roman soldier movies. His dad was puzzled about how Tony had come to know anything about body armor.

"When did you wear these?" his dad asked again, incredulous.

"I don't know, but it was a long time ago. A *loooong* time ago!"

Many years later, while reading a book about ancient Rome, that memory flooded back in a torrent, and Tony knew on that day he had seen himself as a Roman soldier. Tony was mesmerized by the idea of war and battle, and went to great lengths to plot his course of action when met with the enemy while playing war games. He often imagined a different kind of soldier's uniform and type of armor, along with a variety of weapons and diverse terrains. To any casual observer, it would appear that Tony had been given training in the many wars of the world throughout the centuries. However, Tony was operating intuitively from what was already within him, not from anything he had been told or taught.

Tony had always had an affinity for America and a strong emotional connection with World War II. In fact, in his young life, there had been many times when he would find himself flooded with a feeling that he had been an American who fought and died in the Second World War. These feelings were hard to understand and even harder to explain. His family heritage and roots had been planted firmly in Venezuelan soil for hundreds of years. Before that, his ancestors hailed from the Basque country. Still, he held a great love for and loyalty to the United States of America for as long as he could remember. Everything that had to do with America felt like home to him in a way that even his country of birth, Venezuela, did not. Tony loved everything that had to do with America: the American flag, apple pie—all of it. This deep love and affinity for the United States was something none of his other siblings felt nor understood in him.

As Tony grew older and his parents became more confident that he and his brother were able to stay safe while navigating the neighborhood streets, he and Eduardito were allowed out of the house a bit more. One of their favorite pastimes was to play war. Any kind of mock battle or simulated fighting would do. When given the opportunity to direct these playtime activities, Tony often had everyone acting out scenes he had seen flashes of in his mind, as if some magical movie projector had played images of battles in his head. The scenes he envisioned seemed real, and he was so connected to them that he was mystified how they got there. He directed them with such passionate attention to detail as though he were either the world's youngest self-made method actor/director with the most vivid of imaginations, or he was reliving a past-life memory when he was a high-ranking soldier in the trenches with his men.

Christmastime was a month-long celebration throughout Venezuela, with the rich aroma of simmering savory beef, pork, or chicken seasoned with sautéed raisins, capers, olives, onions, and bell peppers for the making of *hallacas* floating on the breezes in entire neighborhoods. The meat would slow-cook for hours until it reached the appropriate level of perfection. Once ready, the stew would be carefully spooned onto maize fashioned into a rectangle, placed in a folded banana leaf, neatly tied with cotton string, and next boiled or steamed.

The making of hallacas was itself a celebration, with every house packed with cheery extended family members and friends. Women were hard at work preparing the featured treat, men busy with the talk of the day, and kids running about as kids do. Each residence was abuzz with activity. Gaita, traditional lively Venezuelan festival music played mostly at Christmas, filled each home with the spirit of the season.

Every family had their own secret way of making hallacas, with everyone confidently asserting that no one made the dish better than their grandmother, mother, or favorite aunt. Good-natured arguments over who made the best hallacas was a constant topic of conversation and a point of family pride.

Christmas and New Year's Eve dinners included other meticulously prepared food, like *pan de jamón* (a puff pastry filled with ham, raisins, olives, and bacon) or chicken salad and *pernil* (leg of pork). These meals were finished with an array of desserts, with panettone bread the most revered.

Much like the time-honored traditions of the elders, the children had forged traditions of their own. These were rituals that adults knew little about yet could have been quickly discovered if their parents had not been distracted by the lively conversations and loud music that drowned out the other less peaceful sounds echoing throughout the neighborhoods.

These childhood traditions would find the kids waiting in anticipation in the weeks leading up to the Christmas season and were spoken about for months after.

Much like the Fourth of July in America, Christmastime in Venezuela was marked by fireworks and firecrackers that made it seem that the entire city was a war zone under siege. Tony and his neighborhood friends loved this time of year so they could participate in a wildly fun yet highly dangerous activity. They would play their usual war games, but instead of rocks or other projectiles, they'd employ fireworks, firecrackers, or cherry bombs hurled as grenades at one another. More than one child Tony knew had lost fingers holding on to an M-80 firecracker for too long.

The kids would devise different ingenious ways of propelling fireworks and firecrackers. Their favorite was a slingshot, which required a bit of expertise and exact timing, but could send a firework half a block. Or when they got ahold of fireworks meant to be shot into the sky, they would seal one end of a pipe and insert the lighted firework. They'd point it at the neighborhood kids, and the newly invented bottle rocket became a useful projectile. On one particularly bad night for the brothers, Tony tried to throw a whistling firework across the street toward another group of kids, but it slipped out of his hand and landed on top of Eduardito's head, burning his hair down to the scalp. They also took to extracting gun powder from the fireworks and making their own devices, which they would leave on an enemy's front porch after lighting them and running off, or seeing how much firepower it would take to blow a manhole cover off the street.

On another occasion, the boys decided to test out the accuracy of their mother's antique cannon, a smaller-than-life-size replica from the 1800s she had purchased several years before while vacationing in Spain. She considered it a piece of art, proudly displaying it in the sitting room.

The antique was a beauty to behold, with its precise attention to detail, oil-rubbed bronze finish, and smooth curves. The cannon was perched atop a carriage of sorts that allowed it to be wheeled from one place to another, just like in battle.

The boys had fired off several explosives that day using the cannon and testing the limits of the bronze antique, pretending they were actual soldiers in battle. Unfortunately, in their excitement, they used a little too much gun powder this time. After lighting the fuse, they waited for the predictable explosion. But the cannon behaved much differently than it had previously. Instead of launching a projectile across the landscape, it made a giant *BOOM*, and then lurched into the air while ripping itself apart. The extra gun powder had turned the toy cannon into a grenade that tore the barrel from the carriage it had been attached to, propelling it high into the air and the same distance forward. The boys' startled gaze followed it upward like a rocket ship leaving a launchpad. As the cannon reached an apex and began its descent, the boys took a quick survey of where they believed the cannon would land and recognized that the situation had just graduated from a minor problem to a major one—it was heading toward other homes and cars parked on the street.

Without a word, both boys sprinted to the site where the cannon was falling. It careened back to the Earth, announcing its arrival with a loud rattling thud, fortunately landing smack dab in the middle of the street in a pile of smoke and molten metal. The boys stood slack-jawed and motionless in front of their mother's treasured possession. Much too hot to touch for many minutes, they were resigned to just stand there out in the open, waiting to be caught red-handed. There they stood, staring mutely at the smoldering mess they had made, contemplating what could have happened to them if the thing had exploded on the ground, or if any of the red-hot metal had fallen on them like a real mortar shell finding its target. They realized they might have lost a limb or been maimed or, worse, killed in an instant.

Waiting for what was left of the cannon to cool down so they could move it were the most torturous minutes the boys had ever spent. They furtively craned their necks to see if any startled neighbors would come running from their houses to investigate. But luck was on their side once again. There were no witnesses. Their only problem now was their mother and what to do with the remnants of her prized possession.

The brothers attempted to conceal the damage to the cannon, tucking its twisted remains in a far corner of the sitting room and placing a couple of chairs in front of it. Many months later, while preparing the home for a dinner party, their mother realized that the cannon was missing. Having not been in this room for some time, she had not noticed its absence. She scanned the room, and in the far corner, she saw the big mangled mess of a cannon hiding behind two chairs. The boys took their punishment without complaint, happy to have it finally out in the open. The burden of the secret had weighed heavily on them both but had only temporarily interrupted their adventurous natures.

Despite the explosion catastrophes, the allure was too strong, and the boys eventually found their way back into danger. One evening, their dad was hosting a dinner party for his friends and Tony's grandfather. Tony and his brother had come into the possession of Roman candles, which everyone was aware you were not ever to hold. Ignoring logic and warnings, Tony, with a group of friends, decided to light the thing and held it carefully, pointing it into the air at a forty-five-degree angle. Glorious sparks flew out to the oohs and ahhs of his friends. All at once, they stopped, which confused everyone, including Tony. He glanced around at his friends, puzzled. Then the Roman candle exploded, releasing a forceful shock wave, almost like a modern-day stun grenade. Tony stood frozen in place, his hand gripped firmly to the bottom of the candle that now more closely resembled a wilted bouquet of flowers than a dangerous firework. Black dust covered his face, hair, and clothing. Unable to move or let go, he could only stand there like a miniature blackened and utterly poor replica of the Statue of Liberty.

Tony's grandfather, having heard the boom and upon discovering what had happened, walked outside to where Tony stood motionless. It was not until his grandfather had peeled each finger one by one off the explosive that Tony was able to bring his sooty arm back down.

Tony's grandfather led him gently inside with an arm draped around his young shoulders, sat him down at a table, and brought him a glass of water.

Tony's father looked on with shock and concern, placed his palm onto his forehead, resting an elbow on the table as he whispered the familiar mantra of many a parent of an adventurous child: "My God, what am I going to do with you?"

Given all the possibilities, it's a miracle that both boys survived with their appendages, hearing, and eyesight intact.

CHAPTER 6

Inspiration

TONY'S FONDEST MEMORIES ARE THOSE OF THE PRIVATE QUALITY time he spent in his father's study, with his dad puffing on his pipe while reading a voluminous collection of children's books to him. Tony's father would act out the different parts and always leave Tony in stitches and wanting more. Among Tony's favorites were the stories of the Brothers Grimm. He particularly enjoyed "Rumpelstiltskin," and always informed his father that if he had been there, he would have rescued the miller's daughter from that tower. This nurturing and encouraging time together was essential. It created in Tony a sense of inner peace and sanctuary as a welcome relief from the danger and chaos of the world that awaited outside.

Tony's father's fine features, fair skin, dark hair, and bright blue-green eyes gave him the appearance of a movie star. He was very fit and athletic, and with his glasses on, to Tony, he resembled Clark Kent. So much so that young Tony thought he was Superman until his dad was able to convince him that he wasn't. Eduardo Arismendi Sr. was an insurance agent, but in Tony's mind, all he heard was "agent," so he readily told his friends that his father was a secret agent, like James Bond.

Mr. Arismendi was wise, soft-spoken, and kind yet charismatic, quite humorous, and joyful of spirit. He was sent to the Cheshire Academy, a Connecticut prep school, as a young man and, for a while, went to a Catholic seminary. He eventually went on to earn a college degree in psychology and always fit right in with Americans. He spoke perfect English, had good manners, and was the product of an upbringing and education that exposed him to literature, art, and music.

Tony's father never raised his voice, disparaged, or talked down to Tony. He would always tell him, "You're smart as a whip, son, so nobody's ever going to be able to fool you or take advantage of you."

When Tony was a little older, his father especially enjoyed talking to him about important issues: philosophy and theology, spirituality, life and death, and the afterlife. When Tony began asking questions and showing a healthy curiosity about spiritual issues, his father took Tony with him to religious sanctuaries that he loved to visit. They went to majestic churches, quiet chapels, monasteries, and other holy shrines, irrespective of what religion they represented. Tony enjoyed the Hare Krishna temple that he had previously wandered into and loved the melodic harmonies of the Gregorian chants at the Christian abbeys.

When his dad saw that Tony was grasping his exposure to different religious and philosophical ideas, taking them in, and asking the right questions, he began introducing Tony to books from his library that Tony would devour. And as Tony grew, his father introduced him to more challenging books, and their conversations became more complex.

And while Tony's mind was absorbing and recording these things, Tony's father would always explain important concepts in a way that the young boy understood.

"So your spirit goes to another place when you die, right, Dad? What happens there?"

His dad would paint a picture that described a pleasant place with a kind and loving God that wasn't all hellfire and brimstone, and helped Tony form vital theological concepts early in his life, always willing to let Tony come to his own conclusions.

He once began discussing the contemporary French religious philosopher, Pierre Teilhard de Chardin, a Jesuit priest and thinker who had many of his writings censored by the church.

Tony stopped him midsentence, informing him matter-of-factly, "I've already read *Le Milieu Divin*. It was fascinating."

At that, Mr. Arismendi went to his bookcase, grabbed the book, and held it out in front of him.

"You read this book?" he asked incredulously, for it was a difficult work, appropriate for someone much older than Tony.

"Yes, Papá."

"And you understood it?"

"Yes. I like the idea that we're all involved in a spiritual awakening together. But I liked *Le Phénomène Humain* better."

His father pulled out another volume of the author's work, an earlier book equally as challenging to read. "And you read this one too?"

"Yes, Father."

His dad stared at the books he held in each hand, then at Tony, trying to figure out how his son was able to read through both volumes with an understanding of the advanced philosophical journeys the author took his readers through. "Well, I'm happy you're interested in such writings, Tony. But let's have a little agreement here that we'll keep the kinds of ideas that Chardin talks about our little secret."

Tony's father was mindful of the fact that some of the edgy Christian concepts contained in the works did not sit well with the presenters of Catholic orthodoxy who taught in Tony's school or with the priests with whom Tony interacted—nor with his conservative grandmother, for that matter. When they would discuss such taboo subjects as reincarnation, Tony's father would always look over his shoulder to make sure Tony's grandmother was not lurking about. Often, he would get up and close the door before venturing into such territory.

"So our little talks don't leave this room, right, son? They're just for you and me alone. Right?"

"Okay, Papá," Tony replied to his father, who gazed upon his son with prideful eyes.

Angela Pardi, Tony's maternal grandmother and godmother, was a tough little woman. She was perpetually in mourning over the death of one relative or another, and permanently wore the *luto*, a black dress with black leggings. When she went out of the house, she added a veil.

On Friday nights, when Tony didn't have school the next day, she would often tiptoe into his room and wake him up. "Antonio. *Levantante*," she would quietly whisper. "Get up."

Sleepy-eyed Tony would follow her back into a parlor in her section of the home and find himself a seat on a sofa. It was a warm and comforting place for him to be, alone with her in her sanctuary amongst her collection of porcelain treasures resting atop crocheted table runners on antique tables. There was an array of family portraits that adorned white stucco walls, and the room had a musty yet not unpleasant odor to it. In the corner of the dimly lit room would flicker a small black-and-white television, its rabbit ear antennae jutting upward. She would welcome Tony to sit next to her on the overstuffed sofa to watch TV. One of Tony's favorite programs was *The F.B.I.*, starring Efrem Zimbalist Jr.

Secretly, he wondered what life was like in the United States and developed a great love and admiration for America. He imagined himself one day in the military or working in law enforcement, like the many members of his extended family.

One evening while watching his favorite show, a station break began to advertise *Hawaii Five-0* coming up next.

Tony turned confidently to his grandmother and blurted out of nowhere, "Someday I'm going to become an FBI agent!"

His grandmother stifled a laugh, not wanting to hurt the boy's feelings. After a short pause, she said, "Well, mijo, you can be anything you want to be."

CHAPTER 7

Separation

THE PERSISTENT BICKERING BEHIND CLOSED DOORS BETWEEN Tony's mother and father became so constant that Tony and his siblings no longer took delight in spying through the keyhole and listening to them. Instead, they would scatter to other areas of the large home to avoid hearing their parents argue. Their mother was unrelenting, and having formed an opinion or staking out a position, she would not let it go even after Tony's father sent up the white flag. His parents tried valiantly but in vain to hold their relationship together. They finally separated, with Tony's father taking up residence in his father's spare condo at the Caracas Country Club.

Tony's paternal grandfather was wealthy in his own right. He owned several houses, land, and business properties, as well as several companies, and had done very well for himself. He was a bold man with reddish hair and clear blue eyes. He was in his sixties and was battling cancer, and although he resisted and fought with all the strength he could muster, he was preparing for the inevitable.

In 1976, Venezuela's economy was booming thanks to a massive influx of governmental spending. Venezuelan oil prices were on the rise, and the country seemed to be flourishing financially. Growth was at its highest, and inequality was at its lowest. The middle class had become quite comfortable, driving fancy cars and drinking the best whiskey. Life was good with no end in sight—or at least, that is what most people thought.

However, Tony's grandfather was not most people. As a young teen, after a tragic accident, he and his brother found themselves without parents and a home. Both boys were adopted shortly after their parent's death by their uncle and raised as if they were his own sons. He too had suffered a major loss when his son drowned in the ocean while away at school. Their uncle was determined to bestow upon these two boys everything he didn't have a chance to give his own son. Knowing that being able to support oneself is of the highest importance, he used every opportunity he had to instill a respect for education, diligent effort, and working smart. Given this knowledge, Tony's grandfather had built his wealth brick by brick.

Studying the financial climate of Venezuela gave him a sinking sense that this bountiful economic period was the calm before the storm. Being an astute businessman, he realized the only way to protect his wealth from the impending collapse of the inflated Bolívar was to invest in a US business to shield himself from the higher inflation and any economic crisis. To explore investment opportunities outside of his country, he sent Tony's father on a series of business trips to other Latin American countries, the United States, and Europe. While his friends and business associates were being lulled into a false sense of security, he was planning his next move. He read the writing on the wall and theorized that Venezuela's economic stability would soon experience drastic change, impacting financial and political stability.

As it turned out, much of the vast holdings of the Arismendi family were later seized by the Venezuelan government during a period of economic downturn in the 1980s.

Tony visited his father at the country club and felt a gnawing unease at observing his dad visiting with a new lady friend. The first time his father's girlfriend dropped by while Tony was there, Tony sensed the connection between the two. While he believed that his dad deserved to have another relationship, he nonetheless felt awkward around the new woman in his dad's life. A disquieting certainty overcame Tony that things had changed, his parent's relationship was over, and the family would never be the same again.

Tony loved his mom and wanted to remain loyal to her, but that became increasingly difficult. His mom would not allow for an amicable relationship with Tony's dad. On a few occasions, she blocked his father from seeing Tony and his siblings and prohibited them from speaking to him on the phone. Things escalated from there. The breakup effectively became a war between two powerful families pitted against one another.

It was not long before Tony's brother, Eduardito, and his mom got into a huge argument that started with something innocuous but intensified to the point that Tony's mother began throwing Eduardito's possessions while screaming at him.

"Get your things and go live with your dad. Get the hell out of here! I know you'd rather live with him anyway! Just go!" she hollered at the top of her lungs, flinging his possessions into a growing pile in front of the door.

A familiar chill ran down Tony's spine as he caught a glimpse of his two sisters peeking out from behind their bedroom door. Tony realized that something had snapped in his mom and, at that moment, naively decided he would stay there out of loyalty and support. His mother was often difficult, but Tony wanted to help as best he could. He would be the man of the family now, he thought.

Then, focusing her gaze on Tony, shook her finger at him and accusatorially shouted, "And you?"

Startled and surprised, Tony quickly defended himself, "I didn't do anything!"

"You want to go live with your dad too?!" she shouted.

"*Cálmese, Mamá!* Calm down, Mother!" Tony retorted, now bristling that he had been unjustly drawn into the fight.

"Why don't you pack your shit and get out of here too? I know that's what you want anyway."

While she continued her rant, Tony's dad, who Tony's mother had called earlier, pulled up in front of the house. Watching his brother load a couple of things into the car, Tony jumped at the chance to get away from the yelling. He sprinted out to him.

"Hey, Dad. Mom's flipped out. She's kicked me out too. Can I come live with you?"

"Of course, son. Go hurry—get your stuff and let's go," his father said without hesitation.

Little did Tony realize that his decision to leave that day would mean that he wouldn't see his mom again for the better part of the next decade. His life was about to change dramatically, and he was about to embark on a journey that would take him to a new country, a new beginning, and a new future.

Tony and Eduardito settled in with their dad and quickly grew accustomed to life at the country club. It was a paradise for them, and as they tried their best to blend in, they somehow managed to keep their teenage mischief to a minimum.

Within a few short weeks, Tony's father asked them, "How would you guys like to go to the United States?"

"You mean like a vacation?" Tony asked.

"Yes, something like that," his father replied.

The boys thought a trip anywhere would be fun and were all for it. But their dad reminded them that their mother must never find out, so they were not to tell a soul. Tony began to get very excited about the great adventure before them, even though he did not speak a word of English.

Tony's father and grandfather were aware that Tony's mother and her family were maneuvering to take the boys back and continued to strive to make Tony's father's life miserable. If they had any hint that a trip was planned, Tony's mom and her family would put a quick stop to it. The two men began laying plans for their escape, with the boys' grandfather taking great care to outsmart his ex-daughter-in-law and her family.

Tony, his dad, and his brother huddled with their grandfather in his study, finalizing every detail of their plans. His grandfather—wizened, coughing, and subtly trembling yet still resisting his disease—had sat the two boys down in his study, turned to them, and said, "You guys are going to America. It will be a great place for you to start over." Only then did the boys become fully aware that their adventure was going to be more than an extended vacation.

With that, their grandfather took out two sets of instructions he had carefully penned in longhand using green ink and handed one to each boy. "Here's a list of dos and don'ts I've prepared for you guys. You're going to a new country. There will be a lot for you to learn. It's going to be good for you, but it may not always be easy. Please keep these notes with you and read them often, and when you do, please remember me." He leaned back in his chair and took a long moment to catch his breath, then continued, "I've lived a long time...and I've had a full life. And thanks be to the Lord, I am at peace. Here are some ideas on things I've learned, and I pray my thoughts will help you grow into the fine young men I know you both can be. Work hard and believe in yourselves. Always stand up for what is right and never quit. Go with God. I love you both."

Tony's grandfather had attended a seminar at the country club hosted by an American. It was a slick presentation aided by a professional slideshow extolling the virtues of his company. His office was based in Salt Lake City, Utah, and the man said the company had a stellar record assisting wealthy clients in Latin America with moving their holdings into the safety and protection of the United States, particularly when local economies became unstable.

Over the course of several weeks, the man ingratiated himself with both Tony's grandfather and father. Since Tony's dad was in the insurance business, it was decided that they would form a new insurance company, which Tony's dad would run. Much of the family wealth could legally and safely be transferred to America through a series of maneuvers involving banks based in Panama. Tony's grandfather was pleased that he was doing the right thing for his son and grandchildren. Tony's father would be assured of an ongoing income for his children in his new life, and perhaps he would somehow persuade his ex-wife to allow Tony's sisters to come to the United States. Best of all, the American's company understood the ins and outs of such matters and could handle all the business and legal aspects of the transaction.

Tony's dad took the boys to the US embassy and arranged for visas. A few days later, their father came for them at school and took them out of class. The boys were exhilarated as they embarked upon their secret mission, and within hours, the three were on a flight to Miami. Tony's father only allowed himself to relax once he was confident the airliner was out of Venezuelan airspace and would not be turning around.

The boys' faces remained glued to the windows for the first part of the flight. It was a cloudless and gloriously sunny day, the Caribbean spread out beneath them in an endless expanse of cyan from horizon to horizon.

They made a game of spotting tiny specks of boats plowing the tranquil sea thousands of feet below. Whoever spotted one first got a point, and like most everything else they did together, they were highly competitive. When they flew over the small island of Bonaire, Tony was reminded of Isla Margarita, where General Arismendi and his wife Luisa Cáceres de Arismendi had risked everything, stood up to the Spanish, and fought the overwhelming Spanish armies to earn freedom for all of South America.

The boys had only flown once before, and excitement and energy were boundless. They expected an in-flight meal, and Tony's hunger became unbearable once the plane was transformed into a restaurant, with a blend of tantalizing aromas infusing the cabin. He savored every bite of his meal, drank as many Cokes as his stomach could hold, and stashed extra bags of peanuts in his pockets for later.

The two brothers spent most of the flight talking cheerfully and sometimes rambunctiously, fueled by the excitement and anticipation of this adventure. Mr. Arismendi spent his time in flight taking in his son's playfulness while revisiting the plans he and his father had mapped out for their journey to America.

At one point, Eduardito mentioned an American movie they had seen at the local theater but couldn't recall the name of. Trying to help Tony remember the film, Eduardito did his best impersonation of the main character's line when asked where he was from. "You remember, Tony, the one where he says"—Eduardito closed his eyes and opened his mouth wide—*"New Yaaark Ciiii…Tayyyy,"* bobbing his head up and down to emphasize each part.

Tony erupted into uncontrollable laughter, almost spitting his drink out across the back of the seat in front of him.

Seeing the annoyance on their father's face did nothing to squelch the boys' laughter and may have fueled it a little unintentionally. A short while later, the random outbursts of giggles had finally calmed down until Tony could hold it in no longer.

He looked sideways at his brother and mimicked the facial expression Eduardito had made, then whispered, "New Yarkk Ciiii…Tayyyyy."

That was it. The boys erupted into laughter and began repeating the phrase back and forth to one another: "New Yarkk Ciiii…Tayyyyyy!" Pretty soon, they had forgotten why they were even saying that phrase. Nonetheless, they were wholly entertained by it.

When it had finally worn out its welcome, their father turned to them and said, "No more, you two. Quit bothering other people!" Mr. Arismendi was embarrassed to see other passengers squirm in their seats, who, if given a choice, would opt for screaming babies rather than two brothers who had worked themselves into a happy frenzy.

A week or two later, their mom would receive a call from their school and learn that they had left the country. Cecilia was devastated at the news and could not believe what had happened. After speaking with her parents, she drove out to meet with her father's attorney. Crying, she relayed the story as the attorney listened and tried to console her.

As she got ready to leave the attorney's office, he said, "Señora, I will move heaven and earth for you and your family, and we'll have your boys back in Venezuela in no time. Just know that at fifteen and seventeen years old, your sons are old enough to know what they want, are not going to be happy you brought them back, and will probably hate you for it."

Before her breakup with Tony's dad, and from the very first time she had met him, Eduardo Sr. had never stopped talking about wanting to move to the US and start fresh. Although she understood his reasoning, it wasn't something that she would seriously consider until years later, when Venezuela's political turmoil was at an all-time high and the economy was on the brink of collapsing. As a mother, she couldn't stand by and do nothing about getting her kids back. Cecilia also knew that if her sons were going to have a future, it wasn't going to be in Venezuela. What the attorney said about the boys hating her reverberated in her mind.

On one of the many late nights she would talk with her mother, she told her, "Mami, things in Venezuela are going from bad to worse, with no end in sight."

Her mother replied, "Sí, mija, isn't that the honest truth!"

Breaking into tears and barely managing to speak, Cecilia said, "And, I have been thinking a lot. I'm going to let them go with their dad and allow them both to find and realize their dreams in Norte America."

Years later, with tears in her eyes, she would often say at family gatherings, "It was the most difficult decision I have ever made in my life!"

CHAPTER 8

The Home of the Brave

It took Tony a few weeks after he landed in Miami to realize that he and his brother had left behind a privileged life. He would also see that, even with the inherent dangers in Venezuela, he and his family had had it pretty good. With an impending reversal of fortune for his father, coupled with learning a new language in a new country, Tony and Eduardito faced a tough period of adjustment.

When Tony first got off the plane, he was captivated by all he saw: a modern air-conditioned airport with polished floors, rows of trendy restaurants, tidy stores of every variety, and well-dressed, well-mannered people. Everyone looked rich to him, and he concluded that the worst place in America was better than the best place in Venezuela.

As Tony walked with his father and brother in a tunnel at the airport, his eyes were drawn to a row of vending machines. Tony's jaw dropped when he saw someone press a button, and a Baby Ruth candy bar slid into a bin to be snapped up. He stopped in his tracks and took a long moment to study the machines. There was only one other time in his life that he had seen a Baby Ruth, when Eduardito had gotten one somehow and brought it home to share with him. It was like gold to the kids, and he recalled how they carefully unwrapped it, admired it for the longest time, then consumed it slowly, bit by bit, savoring every bite as if part of a religious ceremony. When they finished, they lingered, taking turns smelling the delightful scent on the foil wrapper. That Baby Ruth was probably the best thing he had ever tasted, and now he was awestruck that he could get one out of these machines whenever he wanted. He realized quickly why vending machines were not found in Venezuela. As good as the economy may have been, the machines wouldn't last an hour before they were smashed to pieces and looted.

A man walked up to Tony and asked him in English if he had the time, and Tony just stared back at him, expressionless. It was an odd experience for Tony not to understand what was said, and he was instantly mystified. The man asked him a second time, and once again, Tony stood there and stared at the man mutely with an awkward grin.

Tony's father, who had doubled back, broke in and rescued him. "I'm sorry, my son doesn't speak English. It's three thirty-five," he told the man.

The traveler thanked him and continued on his way. Tony asked his dad to get him a candy bar for later, along with a package of Dentyne gum, another delicacy the boys had sampled a couple of times back home but couldn't often find.

In their room in Miami at a Roadway Inn, Tony and his brother were mesmerized by the color television. Tony began changing channels and was delighted to see that there were more than three—the meager number available in Caracas. And when he discovered that American television also showed full-length movies, he figured he'd be spending a lot of time in front of it. He began listening to English and reasoned that the TV would help him learn the language faster.

Tony loved the ice from the ice dispenser at the hotel, a convenience he thought was terrific. You want ice, he thought, and all you have to do is go to this machine, and it comes right out! He bounded into their room carrying a full bucket of ice, an ear-to-ear grin on his face, and shouted to Eduardito, "Man, this place is beautiful! It's the best!"

A Hispanic lady who was tidying up stuck her head out from the bathroom. "What's so beautiful about it?" she asked Tony.

"Everything!"

"You must have just gotten here," she replied with a laugh.

Mr. Arismendi wanted the boys to see some of the country and thought a road trip would be an excellent bonding experience for all of them. Needing to be in Utah for business with the American, they set out onto the interstate and headed cross-country from Miami all the way to Salt Lake City.

To Tony, it was one huge adventure, and he was fascinated by everything he saw. He could not drink it in fast enough. He had not grasped that he was in the United States to stay and still believed that after a few months, he would return to Venezuela and enter military school. But for now, he was in this place where everything was beautiful, clean, and safe. They would encounter all sorts of folks, including riffraff at the gas stations and truck stops along the way. Even those people looked good in Tony's eyes. He kept thinking that even the people who are supposed to be bad don't look so bad.

God, you Americans don't know bad, he thought to himself. *You have no idea what bad is.*

And Tony's father did his best to keep the boys entertained by either rock 'n' roll music cranked up on the car radio or sessions of fatherly advice and encouragement he carefully selected for his captive audience. "You know, you guys can accomplish anything you want," he told them. "Just set your mind to it, make a plan, work hard, and don't give up."

Mostly, Tony and his brother were treated well by the people they encountered on the road. There were occasions, however, when the boys fell under the scrutiny of people trying to figure out where they had come from and what their fair-skinned father, who spoke excellent English without a trace of an accent, was doing with two kids who spoke only Spanish.

As the trio reached Colorado Springs, the boys got their first glimpse of snow. It had accumulated on the ground on either side of the road. Feathery snowflakes collected in small amounts at first, then deepened, covering the ground in a sparkling carpet of white. They had seen the glistening snowcaps that adorned the jagged peaks of the Rockies for miles, but this was their first opportunity to experience snow up close. Their father went on to explain snow, settling on a scientific definition.

"Snow occurs when water vapors in the air freeze before they can turn into water. When the higher air temperature is colder than the ground, little crystals of ice form around particles of dirt in the air. Snow is made up of trillions of snowflakes, and each one can contain as many as two hundred crystals. But you know what? No snowflake is identical to any other snowflake. Isn't that amazing?"

"What does it feel like?" Tony asked.

Knowing that it would be fruitless to try to explain cold and frost to his boys, who had only experienced a warm climate, Tony's father found a safe place to pull over. The boys wasted no time bounding out of the car to romp in this newly discovered frozen playground. The white powder appeared so inviting to Tony that he hurled himself into an abundant snowdrift. He sprang back up with a shriek, then began hurling snowballs at Eduardito. Their father joined in on the melee that ensued, and they soon found themselves laughing while blasting one another mercilessly, until they were forced back into the car by the early stages of frostbite.

Mr. Arismendi got back on the road and cranked the car's heater up to full blast, the boys' fingers and toes held fast to the soothing rush of warm air from the vents.

CHAPTER 9

Salt Lake City

As the travelers reached Salt Lake City, Tony rolled down his window and let a crisp and arid wind rush into the car. The dryness of the air was another new experience for him. The humid, tropical air of Caracas was always soothing to him, and now his lips began to parch in this foreign desert atmosphere. He wasn't sure if he was going to like this new climate.

"Is it always like this here?" he asked his dad from the back seat.

"It gets cold in the winter and hot in the summer. It's dryer here than in Venezuela," his dad said, glancing into the rearview mirror. After he caught Tony's eyes, he continued reassuringly, "Don't worry—you'll get used to it."

But Tony wasn't sure he ever would.

The skyline of the city came into sharper view, and Tony marveled at a collection of skyscrapers that jutted high into an immaculate, cloudless sky. A long row of buildings lined the highway like miniature crafted models set against the backdrop of the soaring snow-capped ridges of the Wasatch Mountains to the city's east. These man-made monuments were no match for the spectacle and grandeur of God's creation in the background, one that stretched for what seemed like hundreds of miles north and south. Tony had never seen a place so neat, clean, and orderly, and he had a hard time accepting that it was a real city and not a vision from a dream.

They soon pulled up in front of a home in a fashionable family-friendly neighborhood. It was a two-story, Tudor-style, dark brick house with arching roofs and plenty of chimneys. A matching brick driveway and walkway cut into a plush fescue grass lawn accented by flowering plants and shrubbery, with groups of mature elm trees tastefully framing the edges of the structure. The home made a statement of modest wealth and stability.

Their new business partner was a burly man with a shaved head. He greeted Tony, his father, and his brother enthusiastically, introducing them to his wife, three daughters, and three sons. Mr. Arismendi's new business partner managed to make his guests feel welcome enough, then insisted that they all pray together to give thanks for a safe journey and to bless their new enterprise.

The American had two of his sons, who were about Tony and Eduardito's age, show them around. Tony followed the boys to their car and watched in amazement as they began loading up their musical instruments and equipment into the back of the 1974 Plymouth Barracuda. One of the boys turned to explain that they were performing that evening and was surprised to see Tony's eyes and mouth wide open in a look of awe.

With Tony's very limited understanding of the English language, the boys tried to communicate with Tony using hand signals, holding up an air guitar and motioning toward the other boys, then the equipment, then the air guitar in an attempt to explain that they were performing that evening.

Tony glanced from one boy to the other, half wondering if anyone else was seeing this. He was about to take a ride with an American rock band of some sort. He nodded and said, "Yes, rock music, very good, is very good."

Tony tried mentioning some of the rock bands he was familiar with, such as Deep Purple. Being Latin, Tony pronounced it "Dep Purpla." The boys seemed perplexed as Tony repeated the name a few times, motioning as if he was playing the air guitar. The boys repeated it over and over, glancing around at one another, trying to figure out who Tony was referring to since he seemed emphatic that they would know.

After a minute or so, one of the boys said, "Wait, do you mean *Deeep Purr-pull?*"

Tony nodded excitedly and said, "Yes! Yes," and repeated the new pronunciation out loud a few times, hoping he could recall it in the future. The boys sang lyrics from a few of the band's famous songs, and Tony sang right along.

Having had a breakthrough and discovering they loved the same music Tony did, the boys high-fived each other and then Tony, who felt he had been accepted into the friendship circle. All at once, the barriers that language had put up, music took down, and it became the bridge of communication. Tony had always been taken by British and American rock music. While the lyrics didn't seem to make much sense, the melody spoke to Tony's heart and moved his soul. He had spent many afternoons tucked away in his room, listening to his treasured records. His records had been like trusted friends he knew inside and out. Friends that he had been forced to leave behind at his mother's house.

Once the equipment was loaded up and secure, the boys piled into the car and headed out, with Michael, the partner's son, at the wheel. One of Michael's friends claimed shotgun, and another sat next to Tony in the back seat. Tony once again found himself in a state of shock and disbelief. These guys looked just like rock stars to him. They wore all the latest clothes, outfits Tony had only seen in magazines or on TV. All three of them had long hair; one guy's was almost to his waist. They wore tight bell-bottom jeans, exotic leather cowboy boots, and wide belts. One had on a tight-fitting sequined vest, and the other two wore long-sleeve rayon shirts with floral designs.

Tony thought it was cool that guys a little older than him were allowed to drive and that Michael already had his own car.

I could learn to like it here! Tony thought. He was operating from a natural high of seeing marvelous new things—a fish out of water. He tried to communicate with a combo of the sign language he was quickly developing and the lyrics to different songs they all liked.

The boy riding shotgun started turning the dial to change the stations. Although most of the boys only heard static as the stations switched, Tony's ears caught a single riff of the guitar's lead run from a song he was familiar with.

He shouted out "American Band!" then began singing the melody: "American band...*da da da da...du du...duh...*"

The boys paused, trying to pick up what Tony was hearing, then looked at each other wide-eyed. "Wow, that's some ear you got man. Far out!"

Later at the school, when the boys did a run-through of Grand Funk Railroad's "We're an American Band," they noticed Tony singing the chorus with them word for word. Tony was in heaven, thinking they sounded better than the original song on the radio. They had Fender guitars, Marshall amps, and a beautiful Ludwig drum kit. They comported themselves on stage with such flair that Tony did not understand why they were not as popular as the English and American bands he liked and followed.

Michael called over a friend, who was president of the Spanish club. The boy asked Tony the question everyone was wondering: How he knew the words to that song? Tony responded that Grand Funk Railroad was one of his favorite bands, and he had taught himself how to play that song, the rhythm part, and a few lead runs.

Tony's paternal grandmother was a concert pianist of some renown, and Tony had developed a passion for music. He collected American and British rock band records, read all the Spanish music magazines that he could get his hands on, and at one time had made a pitch to his mother to study at a musical academy. Fearing that Tony would be swept away by music and not enter the military or politics as she had hoped, Tony's mother dismissed that idea. Tony would have to be content with playing along on an acoustic guitar while listening to songs on the record player he had gotten for Christmas one year. He thought again about the collection of albums he loved and had to leave behind.

One of the boys handed Tony a guitar, and the band ran through the song again with Tony alternating rhythm and lead with one of the other guitarists. Tony had a great time, and his spirit soared. Music always had an uplifting effect upon him. When the song ended, the band members all beamed widely, as did Tony, who sensed their acceptance once again as they nodded their approval.

Tony's family settled into a modest apartment in the northern section of town. He and Eduardito enrolled in a summer English class, and Tony immersed himself in the study of the language. He watched every program on television that he could and developed favorites, including *Sesame Street, Hawaii Five-0,* and reruns of *McHale's Navy, Gomer*

Pyle USMC, and *Gilligan's Island*. Tony became an expert on how to use the *TV Guide* and enjoyed picking out old feature films, especially ones about crime or war. He would hear a new word or phrase and repeat it out loud to himself as he watched. He was determined to focus on losing his accent.

One day, his father sat the brothers down and said, "Boys, you're in America now. I think we should use American names."

Tony and Eduardito considered this a moment and did not object.

"I am going to adopt the name Edward for myself. Antonio, let's start calling you Tony, and Eduardito, you Eddie. What do you think?"

"Sounds okay to me," Tony replied.

"Me too," said Eddie.

Shortly after changing their names, Tony's father was told about a summer-long English immersion class. He signed the boys up promptly, hoping they would meet friends and hone their English skills before the school year began in the fall. Tony continued to devour books, reading them out loud and underlining words that he would look up in first the English then the Spanish dictionary. He would make it a point to use the new word in conversation as soon as he could. Tony became particularly fond of *A Tale of Two Cities*, which he had already read in Spanish but enjoyed even more when he read it again in its original language. He read the rest of Dickens's major works, along with scores of his favorites from other authors he'd already read in his world literature classes.

The way kids played in America was completely different from Venezuela. There, he was blowing things up, pulling out switchblades, or playing war. Here, kids sought out more benign activities. The kid in Tony was reemerging. He'd had one of the first skateboards that had come out in Venezuela and was quite an accomplished skateboarder. When he borrowed his American friends' boards, he easily kept up with them, pulling off ollies, 50-50 grinds, or Indy grabs with the best of them.

He befriended an American named Sean, who was half Hawaiian and wore his hair long. Another long-haired friend was Scott, who was a bit on the wild side. Tony kept his hair short. He began to learn when to draw the line and let his new friends do the kinds of crazy things American teens would do without him, despite their egging him on relentlessly. He was aware that his new American friends often believed they were doing the craziest, riskiest things in the world, and Tony would secretly laugh to himself that these boys had no idea what went on in other places. But he enjoyed being able to play in a carefree environment without looking over his shoulder. He allowed the child in him to reemerge and delighted in being given the chance of a second childhood in this amazing country where it was safe and nurturing and where freedom abounded.

To fund the insurance company venture with their new American partner, the family's money had been placed in a Panamanian bank by Tony's grandfather. Tony's father had encountered some trouble accessing the money and was forced to leave the kids alone while he made a trip to Panama to resolve the situation. It was a short trip, no more than five days. He reasoned that the boys were responsible enough to stay behind in Salt Lake City. He left the boys with food, cash for bus fare, and strict instructions to stick together no matter what. The boys were excited at their newfound independence.

* * *

When Mr. Arismendi returned home from his trip, the boys were still at English immersion class and wouldn't be back for a couple more hours, giving him some time to gather his thoughts. How was he going to tell them that his business "partner" had swindled them and the family fortune was gone? He was having a hard enough time believing it himself. Starting from the moment it really sunk in that all the money was gone, as was his business partner, he had been operating in a haze.

At last, within the confines of his own home, Eduardo allowed himself to process what had happened. The first image that appeared in his mind's eye was the memory of the bank manager's sincere expression of condolences as he explained to him that the account had been closed and the entire fortune had been withdrawn only days earlier. Eduardo spoke with every person at the bank who had any contact whatsoever with the man who closed the account. They each told a very specific web of lies that his "partner" had convincingly woven. After several hours, Eduardo finally came to grips with the understanding that the money was gone.

Never quick to anger and ever the gentleman, as he left the bank, Eduardo offered to hold the door for a young mother whose hands were full, clutching a squirmy toddler on one hip and grasping her other young child by the hand. Right then, he had a flashback from when his boys were around nine or ten. One sunny afternoon, Eduardo had brought the boys with him to the bank to open up small savings accounts. Eduardo wanted to show them how to manage a bank account. He knew it would take some time for them to fully grasp the concept of managing money, but he felt it was essential to give them the experience of independence and the responsibility that comes with it. For a moment, he rested in that memory, back before everything had fallen to pieces with his marriage.

He began to hear a soft echo of a woman's voice: "Tell the man thank you…"

"Thank you, sir," said her child.

And just like that, the sweet memory was gone, and the haze of shock took over.

On the airplane back to Salt Lake City, Eduardo was settling into his seat when a gentleman tapped his shoulder and asked if he would mind switching so he could sit by his new wife. Eduardo did not hesitate even a moment, congratulating the happy couple and moving to his new seat farther back. His kind and polite gestures were so much a part of him that they even operated when he had suffered such a significant loss.

Arriving at his new home in Salt Lake City, Eduardo placed the key into the lock, carefully focusing attention on the key. Sometimes it went in smoothly, but more often than not, it felt like he was attempting to pick the lock to his own apartment. Thankfully, it only took a couple of attempts, and the key turned, unlocking the door with a click. Letting out a sigh, he stepped into the small apartment he now called home. As his eyes scanned the room, he was shaken by the uneasy realization that he did not own one single item his gaze rested upon. When he had lived at his parents' estate, and then his wife's parents' estate, the same was true. But this was different. This was survival, and it was up to him to make sure that they endured. Now was not the time to get caught up in concern—now was a time to find a solution. He sat down at the small kitchen table with a pen and paper, ready to refocus his attention on moving forward and how he was going to provide for his family.

"Main goal: securing a well-paying job with room for growth." He had just lost every penny of his savings and would need to provide for the day-to-day expenses while also rebuilding his savings. The focus now was on having a plan so that when he told the boys the news, they would still feel secure, knowing their dad had already figured out what he was going to do.

∗ ∗ ∗

The boys were happily surprised to see their father home early, but also both knew there was a reason, and it probably wasn't good. Tony's father invited them to join him at the table and asked them all about their time while he was away. He listened intently as the boys spoke about new friends they had met. Only after both Tony and Eddie had shared all their stories did their father tell them the shocking news that the money was gone, but he already had a plan for their recovery. His plan was this: he would travel back to Venezuela to revive his insurance agency business and bring in needed income. The boys would become latchkey kids.

And so they did. They managed to live responsibly, and Tony soon got a job with a lady down the street who hired him to do chores for four dollars a day. Then he got a job as a grocery bagger. He stayed glued to the TV whenever possible, and his English continued to improve.

He was once invited to a friend's home for dinner, and they served Mexican food and Doritos, thinking that was the kind of food Tony was used to and would be pleased by. Tony thought the food was delicious.

"Just like home, Tony?" the father asked. "Like casa?"

Little did they know it was the first time Tony had ever tasted a taco. Then it dawned on him, and he said in his broken English, "No, the food is different in my country. I've never had chips either," Tony said. "They're great!"

It didn't take long for Tony to meet Mexican kids and other Hispanic people he could talk to, and the differences in idioms of Spanish from different places made for more than one humorous situation. Once, he asked a friend to hand him his jacket, but their Spanish was different from his. The correct Spanish for "Give me my jacket" would be *"Dame mi chaqueta."* But for the Mexicans Tony hung around with, "chaqueta" meant to masturbate.

When Tony asked someone to hand him his jacket in Spanish, the young man looked at Tony with a combination of shock and fear. "QUE? NO!!!! LA CHAQUETA!" was the teen's immediate response.

It took a while for Tony to assure the guy that he was not looking for him to do anything other than to hand him his jacket.

Another time, he asked someone from Argentina to *"Dame la cola."* But to the Argentinian, it again had a sexual connotation that left him laughing.

Tony was fortunate to have a band of Hispanics who helped him through his English learning curve. Often they would translate for him and became vital in deciphering what a teacher was saying when he entered school that fall. He would often ask his friends what they planned to do after high school, and they would reply that they were going to get a job as a truck driver or a mechanic. When they'd ask Tony the same question, he would tell them that he planned to go to college and become the president of a company, or maybe join the military and become a general. Or perhaps even an FBI agent. They would laugh at him and look at him as though he were crazy. They would tell him there was no way he was ever going to do that and beg him to tell them what he really intended to do. Tony would hold fast and explain that in Venezuela, everyone in his family was accomplished in some way or another. He saw no reason why he couldn't transfer those family traits to his life in America. He scolded them and encouraged them to set their sights higher, telling them they could achieve more than they envisioned if they would change their thinking.

Tony made it through his first summer in the United States with the limited money his father was able to provide and what he earned on his own. He made up for his inability to speak English by being willing to work hard.

When school started, Tony found himself in a chemistry class with several football players. They displayed an air of privilege and collectively, in an unspoken manner, demanded that their fellow students take notice and show proper respect. One of the football players stood at a chalkboard, trying desperately to solve a problem. Tony sat at the back of the class, having already endured the inquisitive stares of the team as they filed into class earlier. The student at the board finished the equation, then turned to the teacher for approval.

"No, Michael, that's not it. Maybe if you had completed your homework as everyone else did, you could solve that problem," the teacher said.

"I had a game."

"I'm sure you did. Anyone else want to take a crack at this?" the teacher asked.

Tony rose from his seat. The students laughed, then quieted as he picked up the chalk and began writing on the board. Within seconds, he had the problem solved.

"That's correct. Tony—where did you learn how to do that?" the teacher asked rhetorically, knowing Tony wouldn't likely be able to explain. "Well, how about that. It looks like the new student from another country can run circles around some of you."

Tony was only fifteen but already way ahead of the other high school students academically. He had been in a tough college preparatory environment in school in Venezuela that earned him credit for his high school diploma in the US.

A buzzer sounded, and the class was dismissed, some of the students barely concealing their merriment at the star football player being put in his place.

As Tony headed to his next class, he was faced with a gauntlet of football players blocking his way. "Where do you get off showing me up like that, you little shit?!" one of them said as he tried to poke Tony's chest, which Tony deflected. "After school, asshole!" the boy exclaimed as he flounced away, laughing with his buddies.

When Tony and Eddie left the school grounds that day, the football players waited for them. The kid who had called Tony out rushed him with his head down as though to tackle him. Tony stepped aside and caught the kid squarely on the back of the neck with a hammer fist as he went by. He followed swiftly with a left kick to the kid's chin, knocking him down in an instant. The rest of the football players tried to swarm him, but Tony was prepared for that and easily eluded them until Eddie could jump to his side. Together, they took on a group of three or four kids and sent them sprawling in as little time as it took Tony to solve the chemistry equation. It did not take long after that encounter for the word to spread about Tony and Eddie's fighting ability. They never again had any problems with kids picking on them at school.

CHAPTER 10

"Are You Gonna Finish Those Fries?"

TONY AND EDDIE, TWO FISH OUT OF WATER, WERE NOT WITHout their admirers. Some of the local girls found them both exotic and attractive. One time, the boys' father played a triple role of chaperone, driver, and interpreter on a double date the boys had with two beautiful young ladies from school. During the forty-five-minute drive to Bridal Veil Falls, in nearby Provo, Mr. Arismendi filled the girls' heads with all manner of good things about his boys.

"They are both very smart, and they work very hard. They do karate and aren't afraid to stick up for themselves," he told the girls. "They're good kids, and they'll learn English in no time."

Once at their destination, their father slipped them both money and advised the boys what to buy for their dates. He kept talking on the return trip and must have said the right thing. By the end of the day, Tony and Eddie were holding the girls' hands firmly in theirs.

* * *

Mr. Arismendi began showing signs of the stress he was under. He had lost the family money, was dealing with the imminent death of his father, and was struggling to raise his two sons in a new country. Further, his visa was set to expire, and he wasn't sure if he should return to Venezuela or continue to try to make a new life in America. In an effort to create community, he tried to encourage Eddie and Tony to join the Mormon Church as he had done. The boys took the required classes and gave serious thought to making the final steps of baptism. After all his efforts and spending so much time and energy trying to reinvigorate his business in Venezuela, their father finally surrendered to the possibility that he needed to expand his job search beyond Venezuela and Utah and start thinking outside the box.

Not too long after this realization, while attending a community event at church, Mr. Arismendi met a beautiful woman, Helen, who was sixteen years his junior and originally from Minnesota by way of California. He was struck by her beauty and felt something stirring within him that had been sleeping soundly for quite some time. The longer he spoke with her, the more he became captivated by her quick wit and easy laughter, qualities that seemed rooted in a genuine kindness he had rarely seen. It wasn't just that it was easy being with her; she made him feel easy about life and all its challenges. She had a way about her that acknowledged the hardships and honored the hopeful. She was an angel that had somehow wandered into his life, and he hoped that she wouldn't wander back out.

He marveled at how magnificent the human spirit is, that a downtrodden soul can be jolted back to life just by another person's presence. All boyhood excitement and nervousness he once believed he had outgrown returned. It was an instant connection between them, and within months, they were talking about marriage and planning a life together. It was not long after that they exchanged vows, both having found the true love of their lives.

After exhausting all potential business and career opportunities in Utah, Tony's father began focusing his efforts on finding work closer to where Helen was raised and where her family still resided in Southern California. Knowing how important family is and seeing how close Helen was to her loved ones, Tony's father began to formulate a plan.

As a less disruptive alternative to moving to a new place and starting school afresh, they decided that the boys would stay in Salt Lake City to finish high school. Tony's father had already taken all the steps to lower expenses by moving them to a cheaper apartment, and he believed he would be able to provide for and support the boys from afar while he searched for work in California. One thing was for sure—he would not be able to provide for them if he stayed in Utah.

***

The boys were now on their own, staying positive through the transition. The bus ride to their school from the new apartment was at least a half hour ride, sometimes longer. From the bus stop, the boys still had another mile to cross before they caught a glimpse of their school on the horizon. They could tell whether they needed to sprint the final five blocks just by the angle of the sun's reflection off the tall glass windows that flanked the cathedral-like building. A large clock resided like a jewel on a crown at the very top of the building. The boys rarely had time or food for breakfast before their long trek and instead waited until lunchtime for nourishment.

Their father had a difficult time supporting two households, money soon dwindled, and the boys were forced to find other places to live. Eddie had a girlfriend, Cheryl, whom he would eventually marry, and her mother invited him to live in a spare room. Tony's father had arranged for him to move in with a friend's family, but that situation did not work out for long, and he soon found himself homeless. Tony didn't want to reveal his living situation to the teachers at school and feared being placed in a foster home, taken away from all the freedoms he had come to love. Tony managed as best he could. Keeping his part-time job as a grocery bagger, he managed to find enough abandoned food in the break room to survive. Or he'd move around the cafeteria at school and collect food in bags to save for later.

"Are you gonna finish those fries?" he'd ask. "How about the rest of that burger?"

He would sleep at friends' houses whenever possible, but he spent too much time alone on the street. He got skillful at following cars into underground parking garages, and when the owner left, he'd spend a few hours sprawled out atop the warm hood. One night, the temperature dropped to twenty-two degrees, and Tony was forced to try the door handles of cars to see if any of them would open and allow for a sheltered space to rest.

Tony somehow managed to stay in school and even played on the high school soccer team. Tony also became close with a friend he had met over the summer in the English immersion class—Francesco, a boy of Italian descent from Peru. The two became fast friends, and Tony was soon invited to stay in the basement of Francesco's uncle's home. Francesco's uncle, through marriage, was Mr. McCleve, a tough World War II vet full of bravado and war stories. The older man took a liking to Tony, and they soon bonded. Tony loved the man and never tired of listening to his accounts of battles he had endured and missions he had accomplished. The basement room was musty yet comfortable. There was a firm couch that served as Tony's bed. There was also a record player, a lamp, and not much else—but to Tony, it was a palace and a warm place to call home.

Mr. McCleve was an angel who came along for Tony at the right time and to whom Tony was eternally grateful.

Tony and Francesco would sit for hours, with Tony spellbound by Mr. McCleve's war tales. One time, he recounted a night when his encampment was overrun by the Japanese, who had captured several Allied soldiers in a small outpost. Mr. McCleve had pulled the pin on a grenade, ready to heave it at the enemy. At the last second, he realized that they were overrun, and tossing it would give away his position, along with that of two fellow soldiers with him. So they decided to stay hidden under a disabled Jeep and wait for daylight before making their next move. Midstory, Mr. McCleve got a phone call and was unable to finish his tale. Obviously, the man had made it, but Tony often wondered exactly what had happened. He would have to wait thirty years to hear the rest of the story.

A high point came in April, during the end of Tony's first and only year of high school. Tony returned to his basement dwelling and noticed two envelopes that Mr. McCleve had neatly placed on a stand next to the couch. His father had sent him a birthday card with ten dollars in it. There was also a card from his mother. He was surprised to have heard from his mom—and then thought he had died and gone to heaven when he saw that she had sent him forty dollars. Although he had figured out how to sew up the holes in his old clothes, he badly needed new ones. He was meticulous in keeping them clean, so at first glance, no one would detect his financial condition. He promptly went out and bought a few things along with a new pair of white Adidas tennis shoes to replace the ones that were literally falling off his feet. Tony was grateful to his mom and began to correspond with her and his sisters, who were overjoyed to hear from him. In those days, letters from the US would take two to three weeks to arrive in Venezuela and vice versa. He was careful not to say much in his letters about his life and circumstances, and was always happy to hear from them.

Tony continued to impress his teachers at West High School with his determination and intellect. He became very popular in chemistry and math class. Whenever there was a test, fellow students would crane their necks to copy his answers. Tony would always bring obscure yet relevant esoteric angles into almost any discussion. He was able to remember exact quotes and recall obscure facts, like the name of German officer Colonel Von Stauffenberg, who was one of the instigators of the plot to kill Hitler.

Or he would hear a particular passage and say, "Oh, that's Emerson."

He got looks from his teachers who sometimes wondered aloud, "You can barely speak English. How could you possibly recognize that's Emerson?"

Tony would just smile and shrug unassumingly.

He was a history buff as well, and whether it was European history or American history, Tony was a walking encyclopedia. Often, his teachers would put a word up, and Tony would immediately recite its Latin root. Tony had thoroughly impressed his teachers. Several had taken him under their wing and given him extra attention. The school's assistant principal, Mr. Blackhurst, periodically came to Tony and notified him that he was no longer a freshman but a sophomore or junior or senior. He didn't understand the terms, as they were not used in Venezuela. At different points, he was pulled aside by the school staff and directed to take various tests, along with the ACT and SAT.

Never before had the yearbook staff been tasked with the continuous updating of a student's grade level. In fact, it had caused the editors so much confusion that when the yearbook was finally sent to print that spring, the committee had moved him around the yearbook pages so many times that they forgot to add his name back into the index. Toward the end of the school year, and after the final edit had been sent to press,

Tony was once again surprised when Mr. Blackhurst told him he was now a senior and would graduate with his brother in the class of 1978. Tony was fifteen and almost done with high school.

West High School Graduation Day, 1978

Eduardo and Helen came to Eddie and Tony's graduation ceremony. Eddie was stable and happy in his relationship with Cheryl, so it was difficult for him to agree to move to Southern California to live with his father and new stepmother. But Cheryl was bound for college, so it was decided that Eddie would leave Salt Lake City with them. The boys piled into their dad's car and began another chapter in their lives.

CHAPTER 11

The Friendly City

EDUARDO DROVE THE BOYS TO CALIFORNIA, WHERE HE AND Helen had found a two-bedroom apartment in Bellflower, a small city in the Los Angeles suburbs close to where Helen's family lived in Lakewood. He filled the boys with praise that they had stuck to it and succeeded against all odds.

"That's what we do, hijos. We Arismendis do not quit. God puts an obstacle in front of you, and you either go right through it or figure out a way to go over it, around it, or under it if you have to. But failure is not in our vocabulary. I'm so proud of you guys I could cry," he said tearfully. "And so is your abuelo. And it's a good thing he's still here to see this. He's extremely pleased and feeling well enough to make the trip to come see us!"

That was fantastic news to the brothers, who loved and respected their grandfather and longed to see him again while his health allowed. Their dad had been working hard to recover from the financial blow they had taken at the hands of the American who had swindled them.

Tony's brother asked, "Papa, what's going to happen to the guy who took our money? Will we ever get it back?"

"Mijo, the honest truth is that I don't think we'll ever see him or the money again," he answered.

Mr. Arismendi was hurt but determined not to allow the actions of one bad person to dictate their fate and was confident he would find a way to overcome. He approached their economic recovery with his usual kind nature and grace, and the boys didn't let the incident sour their outlook on America or life in it.

As they rolled into the city for the first time, Mr. Arismendi pointed to a large sign that proclaimed, "You are now entering Bellflower, the Friendly City." He told the boys he looks at that sign every time he passes, and he still can't figure out, "What's so friendly about this place?!"

The boys cracked up with him, and he repeated what he'd said in English so Helen would be in on the joke, and her laughter confirmed her agreement with the sentiment.

As Tony settled in, he came to think that Bellflower was a friendly and nice enough place to live, although it took him a long time to get used to the not-so-nice constant nuisance of the noisy, omnipresent helicopters circling overhead in search of bad guy after bad guy. Their penetrating searchlights lit up the night sky, and officers on the helicopters would frequently use their loudspeakers to issue commands. It often felt like a war zone to Tony, but he figured they were doing a needed job and tried to tune them out.

The climate in Southern California was much closer to what Tony was used to in Venezuela and therefore more agreeable than that of Utah. He still preferred the humidity of the tropics and not the tolerable dry heat everyone raved about.

The apartment building they lived in was beige, two-story, clean, and nicely landscaped, built in a U-shape around a grassy courtyard. Its residents were a mix of working-class families, singles, and the elderly, and everyone got along well. Tony's dad helped him find a job as a grocery bagger, and he began his second stint as a box boy. He was pleased he could help out financially and was happy that he didn't have to be constantly on the lookout for discarded food for survival.

One day while walking home from work, Tony happened upon a karate studio in a quaint business district where a collection of mom-and-pop shops adorned both sides of the street. Most shops were in one-story structures built in the 1920s and '30s, with large display-window storefronts and canvas awnings to screen out the abundant California sunshine. Tony peered inside the gym, and through the thick plate glass window, he watched a class in progress. His curiosity caught the eye of the owner, who motioned him in. The two hit it off right away. Tony told him about his training in Venezuela under Shoko Sato. By coincidence, the instructor had once met the former champion at a tournament.

Before long, the instructor loaned him a uniform and invited Tony onto the floor to spar with some of his students. Tony immediately impressed him with his martial arts prowess and was invited to join. When Tony told him he had no money to spend on classes, the sympathetic owner offered Tony free enrollment in return for tidying up the studio. The owner thought Tony would be smart advertising for his dojo. There weren't too many skinny sixteen-year-olds around who could move like Tony, and there were plenty of teens lacking in confidence who would find inspiration in watching Tony work out. The owner knew that kids would conclude if Tony could achieve a high level of proficiency, so could they.

Tony had arrived in California during a time when the surf craze among teens along the coast was peaking. Seal Beach, with the closest good break, was a mere thirty-minute drive from Bellflower. Tony made friends with some surfers who lived in his neighborhood and was soon invited to join them. They would make daily treks to Seal, Sunset, or Huntington Beach. But when the surf was up, they pooled enough gas money to travel north to Zuma or south to Trestles. On these days, they would get up before dawn and find themselves competing for waves as the sun came up. They'd stay out all morning until hunger called them in, and they'd take a quick break for a burger or a sandwich and stay out in the water until the late afternoon winds came up and the waves became too blown out to offer an enjoyable ride.

Tony liked everything about the beach scene: the hot sand and the relentless sunshine imparted a feeling of aliveness and comfort. The blue cresting waves crashed upon the shore in organized sets, their spray releasing the overwhelming and refreshing scent of a primordial soup that Tony found alluring. The constant, irrepressible shrieks of joy emanating from children and adults alike filled his ears, making him feel wholly present and part of it all. The playful breezes ruffled hair and lifted the seagulls and pelicans to great heights or allowed them to skim effortlessly above the water's surface in search of food. When he walked along the seashore dressed in his orange board shorts and flip-flops, he felt a sense of freedom he had never experienced. The warmth of the sun and the salt water gave his hair and bare skin a welcome sheen. He felt no harm could come to him there.

The few times his dad had taken the family to the seashore in Venezuela, they all knew to be continually on guard—not from creatures who inhabited the water or from dangerous surf but from their fellow man. There, muggers, thieves, or abductors could appear from anywhere and in an instant change the course of one's life. Here, he could be at peace and let go, allowing himself to merge the pleasant physical sensations with an inner sense of well-being and gratitude to God, who had taken him to this paradise on Earth. The joy he felt was like what he experienced marching and chanting with the Hare Krishnas or the out-of-body experiences he'd had while praying.

In these moments of reverie, he gave thanks. He felt gratitude and genuinely appreciated how his journey had taken him to a better life and to this playground that attracted all kinds of people from various places and diverse social and economic strata, who shared an enjoyment of the water, sand, sun, and fresh air. Tony was sure this was the best place in the world to live, and the simple act of walking on the beach, no matter how many times he had done it before, made him feel alive and refreshed and lifted his spirits to soaring heights.

His friends lent him a surfboard, an out-of-style Dale Velzy longboard, full of dings and patches that he learned to wax. He would carry it proudly under one arm to the water's edge. He quickly mastered how to charge into the bubbling water and plop atop his board, thrusting its tip into the bottom of an incoming wave, then pop through to the other side. Tony thought busting through a big swell was fun enough, and even if he never learned to stand on the board, he'd be fine with the roller-coaster effect of making it through the front of a wave and gliding down the backside while clinging onto the edges of the board with both hands.

He learned how to paddle out, prone at first, then while kneeling, balancing on his board until purple walnut-sized knobs appeared just below his knees. They were painful at first, but Tony wore them as a badge of honor, as all surfers had knobby knees. A glance at someone's knees would reveal who the real surfers were.

Tony delighted in his accomplishment the first time he was able to stand up on a board, but his reverie soon ended when he was abruptly thrown off and cast into a churning whitewater break. He relaxed and allowed himself to bob to the surface, turned toward land, and watched his board race shoreward atop a bubbling torrent of foamy water before planting its skeg firmly in the sand some seventy-five yards away. Most serious surfers did not yet use surfboard leashes, and Tony's crowd shunned them, calling them "kook cords" that were reserved for wannabe surfers.

As Tony swam in, he wore a grin from ear to ear, relishing in his accomplishment and only too happy to grab his board and paddle out again. He was soon cutting rights and lefts, and by the end of that summer, he could ride the crest of a good-sized wave, cut back up the face again, and then reverse back down, then up and out the backside. He could "hang five," creeping to the nose of his board and gingerly jutting five toes of his left foot over the tip of his board while balancing up front. He almost pulled off "hanging ten" a few times, but no matter how much he leaned back, he would lose his balance and wipe out.

In those days, West Coast teens amid surf culture were sure they were at the center of the universe—everything else revolved around them. They were the "beautiful people" who had the best sport and lived in the best place. They had the best clothes, the best hairstyles, and the best cars, and anyone who wasn't like them was "out of it." Tony was beginning to believe this too. His dad bought him a pair of Ray-Ban-like aviator sunglasses, chromed on the outside like the ones Strother Martin's character, Captain, wore in *Cool Hand Luke*. Like the other surfers, Tony thought he was definitely one of the coolest kids in all of Southern California.

At the beginning of the summer when Tony first started surfing, he had no tan on his pale skin. But the more he went to the beach, the darker his tan became. By the end of the season, he had gotten considerably darker and come to realize that there was a definite correlation between the color of his skin and the way he was treated by other people. He tried not to let it bother him. He figured this was just the way it was in America, and he'd be able to overcome that too.

He'd always managed to get around on foot or the bus. But he eventually realized he needed his own car since everyone in LA drove, and getting around was increasingly difficult without wheels. Further, he had enrolled at Cerritos College, a small community college in Norwalk, and would need transportation when he started classes that fall. Tony's dad took out a loan for $1,000, which Tony agreed to repay out of his paychecks from the supermarket. Tony scoured the newspaper ads and found an all-black 1965 Mustang with a 289-cubic-inch engine that he fell in love with—sight unseen. Tony called the owner after work and found out it was still available, but there were several other people interested in it. He was confident such a find would be snapped up by another buyer and tried to convince his dad to take him to see it that evening. Mr. Arismendi warned him it was probably not the best idea.

"Mijo, it isn't smart to go look at a used car at night. Let's wait until morning," he said.

But Tony insisted. "Dad, I want that car! It's not going to be there tomorrow!"

When they pulled up to the address Tony had been given, his eyes were immediately transfixed on a sleek black Mustang bathed in the soft light from a streetlamp. The vision of his dream car enveloped in a halo only further convinced Tony that the Mustang was meant to be his.

When he managed to pry his eyes away from the most beautiful car he'd ever seen, he glanced up to the house. He only partly registered how unusual it was that the heavy security screen front door had three deadbolt locks.

What could possibly be so valuable inside that this guy would need that many locks on his door? Tony thought in passing.

"Okay, Tony," his dad said discreetly. "Let me do all the talking. And the first thing we need to do is to look the car over before anything else. Okay?"

Tony replied with an eager nod.

"Bueno. Now let's see about this car you've fallen in love with!"

As they approached the hefty screen door, a loud, booming bark that could only have come from a massive scary dog startled them both. The screen door clanged as a heavyset bearded man began unlocking each deadbolt one after another. Tony now understood why his father had cautioned him about buying a car after dark, and a twinge of concern briefly overtook him, then quickly vanished when he glanced over his shoulder at that beautiful fastback out there on the street.

As the man opened the door, Mr. Arismendi introduced himself. "Good evening, sir. I am Eduardo, and this is my son, Tony. I believe my son spoke to you on the phone earlier?"

The three men walked to the car while Tony's dad asked more questions about it. Tony walked around it, still taken in by its beauty.

Noting Tony's enthusiasm, the man deftly opened the driver's side door, reached in, and flipped the visor down, releasing a set of keys into the palm of his hand. Holding the keys up as a hypnotist would, the man took measure of Tony's dad, and then his eyes shifted back to Tony. He squinted, then said in a Southern drawl, "By the looks of things, I believe this boy here is rarin' to take 'er out for a spin."

Not understanding what the man meant, Tony stood there for a moment until he realized the man was offering him a chance to test-drive his dream car.

"Well, all right then, boy, get on in, and she'll show you what she's got!" The man tossed the keys to Tony.

Once inside, he took a long time to savor the moment. He slid one hand over the slick vinyl upholstery that felt like leather to him. Tony ran his fingers over an emblem embossed on the back of the passenger's bucket seat, a galloping herd of horses, thinking that little touch was very cool indeed. He clasped the steering wheel with both hands and wondered,

Is this real wood? It sure seemed like it to him. He studied the five-dial instrument panel on the dash and thought it belonged in a rocket ship instead of a car. Grasping the gearshift lever, he cocked his head, anticipating the throaty roar the engine was sure to make when he cranked it up. Tony was ready to run.

He carefully glided the key into the ignition switch, but the key would only go halfway and no further.

He glanced up at the man quizzically, and the guy said, "Oh, she's a little persnickety there. Just jiggle 'er a little bit, and she'll go."

Tony fiddled with the key and finally got it to turn, then heard the glorious sound of the Mustang's V-8 engine as it came to life.

After a couple of times around the block and a quick negotiation, the car was his. Tony went to bed that night with visions of his new car racing in his head. When he woke up, he hurried out to admire it in the morning light, his dad right behind him.

When he saw it, his heart sank, his face turned pale, and he broke into a cold sweat. The bright morning light illuminated the shiny exterior of Tony's car. The black paint had been applied with a paintbrush in bold strokes that left ridges and resembled tar more than paint. Tony tried to say something but couldn't get it out.

His dad stifled a laugh.

Helen came out to see the dream car Tony had been gushing about all night and put two hands over her mouth, then slid a hand over the hood. She glanced from the car to Tony and Eduardo and gave a warm smile. "You know, Tony, this car looks like a real piece of art!" she offered in her good-natured Minnesotan accent, then patted Tony's shoulder and headed back inside.

Tony walked around the Mustang, inspecting it from different angles. The more he studied the paint, the more he convinced himself that it did look like some kind of work of art. He began to see the night sky of a Van Gogh in the textured strokes. Of one thing he was sure—no one in his crowd had a car that looked anything like his.

Eager to show his new purchase to his friends, he met a buddy at a local drive-in. His friend's car, a 1972 yellow Mustang Fastback, had huge slicks on the back wheels and a bigger engine than Tony's. When he challenged Tony to a race, Tony knew he didn't have a chance against it. But they decided to run anyway and headed out to a deserted road.

Tony's three friends climbed in with him, and after a rolling start, they hit it. The yellow beast charged ahead, its massive back tires spinning wildly, leaving the cool night air thick with a cloud of billowing white smoke. Tony knew he couldn't keep up, but he was itching to see how fast his car could go. He hit about seventy miles per hour when they reached a railroad crossing atop an incline—in effect, a huge speed bump. Tony's car catapulted skyward, all four wheels getting air like in a movie.

The Mustang slammed down, and Tony heard the painful thud of the car's U-joint ripping off. He glanced in his rearview mirror and saw it skipping down the road behind him. Suddenly, there was another loud thump, and pieces of the floorboard disintegrated right from under them. Everyone lifted their legs in shock, knowing there was now nothing between them and the rough asphalt that shot by beneath their feet. Tony clutched the steering wheel in a death grip, praying that the car would stop. Thankfully it began to slow, but just before coming to rest, Tony heard one last shriek from the dying car—the ripping of metal as the Mustang split in half. He glanced over his shoulder to see his two terrified buddies, who'd been a few inches behind in the back seat, now in half a car.

When the dust settled, Tony leapt out of what was left of his car and made sure everyone was okay. They were. But the Mustang now sat in two sections without a floorboard. His painted-over dream car was rusted out and broken in half, just like his heart, with its parts strewn all over the road.

Once his friends got over their initial shock, they grabbed their stomachs, laughing as they ribbed him mercilessly for having bought such a piece of junk. Tony failed to see any humor in it. All he could think of was the fifty-dollar monthly payment he'd have to make to his dad, with nothing to show for it except a very expensive lesson.

CHAPTER 12

College

After the death of the short-loved Mustang, Tony and his father scraped enough money together for Tony to buy another car—this time a 1969 El Camino from one of Tony's friends. It was a candy-apple-red, clean, and low-slung ride that rolled a sedan and a pickup truck into one. It had only an in-line six-cylinder engine that made the car painfully slow and ended Tony's racing days. But it was reliable transportation, and it got Tony to and from Cerritos College, where he took an array of classes that interested him, with no particular focus on a four-year degree.

Tony's candy apple red 1969 El Camino

He pledged a fraternity. At the keggers they held to celebrate any day that ended in *y*, Tony would toss out the beer foisted upon him when no one was looking and fill his glass with a soft drink. Fellow pledges and members would marvel at his ability to drink everyone else under the table but not get drunk himself.

His primary motivation for wanting to join was to meet the young ladies that the frat attracted, but he quickly discovered most of the coeds had little interest in a thin sixteen-year-old two to three years their junior. He endured the silly rituals of pledging that culminated with what he considered a ridiculous, egocentric, and cruel "Hell Night." At a mysterious candlelit ceremony that followed, he learned a special handshake and a secret call he could utter to his fellows at the slightest hint of distress, which would summon his brothers to come to his aid. He had been accepted into the group.

Then he promptly quit. Tony concluded these guys were not his kind of people and figured he'd be better off making his own friends. He focused on school and immersed himself in his studies, preferring the insular pursuits of a scholar over the social life of a frat boy. He preferred sitting alone in the sun on his beach chair in the grassy courtyard of his apartment complex while he did his required reading.

There was a family of four who lived downstairs, directly below the Arismendi apartment. The two families kept their distance, as the parents of the family downstairs held unabashedly racist views, blaming minorities for taking their jobs and ruining the country. Their oldest child wore proudly an arrogance imparted by his parents. He was older than Tony and walked around with a chip on his shoulder and his nose in the air. He was a buffed-out, good-looking blond kid with his own car and a pretty girl always on his arm. Tony often encountered him and would greet him with respect and neutrality; both knew there would never be friendship between them. And, Tony hoped, no hostility either.

Tony could not detect overt disdain on the other boy's part until, one day, Tony was reading a textbook in the courtyard when his neighbor passed by hand-in-hand with a girl as they walked toward the apartment. Tony had parked his El Camino in front.

It caught her eye, and she said, "Nice car," out loud to herself.

Tony overheard her and responded with a polite, "Thank you," just as he had done many times before to anyone who offered a compliment. The El Camino was the most valuable thing he had ever owned, and he felt a real pride of ownership.

As the couple passed, Tony smiled appreciatively.

But in response, his neighbor uttered in disdain, "Why don't you go back to your own fucking country?"

Tony shot him a confused look. Then the guy reached down and flipped the book out of Tony's hand.

Tony leaped to his feet, his Venezuelan switch now triggered, and yelled, "What did you just say?"

"You heard me. Why don't you go back to your own fucking country? You want me to kick your ass right here, right now?" the kid barked back, wanting to impress his girl.

Their voices attracted everyone's attention. Window blinds parted, doors opened, and startled neighbors began to peer out of their windows to see what the commotion was all about.

The muscular kid was a wrestler from the local high school, and he did what wrestlers usually do: he shot in with both arms in front of him, trying to take Tony down in a classic double-leg takedown. When Tony recognized he was charging, he moved to his right, to the outside of the boy's extended left arm, and neatly deflected it with a well-timed up-down block. The wrestler then turned toward Tony and tried to grab his elbow with his right hand, leaving his chest uncovered, presenting just enough of an opening for Tony to plant a right snap kick directly to the boy's solar plexus. The blow caught the boy cleanly, and the kid's reflexes straightened him up, leaving his face exposed. Tony delivered a combination of punches, then caught him with a spinning heel kick that sent him flying backward onto his rear end.

Just like that, the fight was over. The kid sat there stunned, having no idea what just happened. His companion oscillated from asking him if he was all right to turning and screaming profanities at Tony.

The boy's mother came out and threatened to call the police. Tony's father rushed out to break up a fight that was already over. Ever the voice of reason, he was able to sort things out with the boy's family as well as with the apartment manager. Mr. Arismendi was able to convince everyone that Tony was only defending himself and promised it wouldn't happen again. From that day on, the boy went out of his way to avoid Tony, making sure he waited until he had left for the day before leaving for school himself.

It was about this time that Tony began working at Knott's Berry Farm, the well-known amusement park in Orange County, California. He was initially hired to keep the grounds clean as a sweeper, but when the staff supervisors became aware of his skill with languages, he was promoted to a group tour guide, one of the most coveted positions in the park. Tony grew to love his job. He made a lot of friends, and what made the job even better was that the staff and managers treated their employees like family. They knew all their employees' names and kept the break room stocked with goodies.

Later that year, Tony's ailing grandfather managed a trip up from Venezuela, and it would prove to be the last time that anyone in the family was able to spend time with their revered patriarch. They all crammed into the small apartment. It was by no means an inconvenience—rather, an opportunity to enjoy time together and reaffirm the love they had for one another.

Seeing his grandfather in such a state was sad for Tony at first. The unspoken and immutable fact was that they were saying goodbye, and that reality hung in the air and colored the family's interactions. But this time also provided an excellent opportunity for Tony and his dad to go on walks or drives and discuss the end of life and what may lie after. Tony found it helpful to talk about such things with the person who helped him formulate his worldview and spirituality.

Tony's father admitted that losing his father was going to be one of the hardest things he would ever go through. But Mr. Arismendi told his son that he had arrived at a place where he could accept his father's passing as the way things are. If he were to resist and fight the inevitability of it, he said, he would be separating himself from being present in a perfectly normal transition that every person and every family on Earth must confront at one time or another. He said that he was no different than anyone else, and he would manage what he had to endure.

"One thing I am certain of is that on this magnificent planet we call Earth, there are trillions and trillions of different life forms in existence at any one time," he said. "And every single one of them moves in and out of existence on their own time schedule. Maybe a certain bacterium only lives for seconds, yet a tree, like the sequoia, can live for a few centuries. But eventually, we all must pass from the realm of the living into the dead. Nothing escapes this reality.

"We are given a limited number of days, hours, seconds, and then inevitably, we pass. The wise man accepts this graciously and still seeks—and finds—joy. The fool fails to grasp this principle, fights it, and will never find happiness, for he will look for it in all the wrong places and never experience internal peace.

"We can never prove that there's life after death. Those of us who believe that our soul and our consciousness endure take that on faith, which sometimes can be as compelling as empirical evidence. I, personally, have always felt that way. And this I felt long before I was exposed to such things as Catechism class or metaphysical writings. So I take comfort that death is merely a transition into another life.

"Sure, I'm going to miss my father terribly, but I feel in my gut that I will remain close to him in my heart and still be able to communicate with him—just not with words. Love never vanishes. If I were to resist the way things are, it would be as pointless as trying to hold back the tide."

Once comfortable accepting the inevitability of the natural process their loved one was going through, the family's interactions became a heartfelt send-off. When they wheeled the frail, old man to the gate of his flight returning to Venezuela, the family embraced him with more tears of joy than sadness.

Tony stayed in Bellflower until he was eighteen, piling up more credits than most students. Eddie had enrolled at Long Beach State and was well on his way to earning one of the many graduate and postgraduate degrees he would eventually hold. Helen had gotten Tony's father into the Mormon Church in a more committed way, and she and Mr. Arismendi influenced Tony to enroll at Brigham Young University.

He struggled through his first winter back in Utah, a particularly cold one. He quickly discovered his California clothes were just not suitable for the frigid weather, but he made do as best he could. He shared an apartment with five other students, three to a room. It was a difficult and inconvenient way to live, but Tony again made the best of a less than ideal situation.

Tony was working out a lot, still doing martial arts and calisthenics along with light weights, and his skinny frame began to expand to the toned body of a man. He was now six two and carried his 175 pounds well. And he became aware of a novel and pleasing realization: women were starting to notice him. In his recent past, girls would pat him on the head and ask to borrow his class notes. But now they appeared to be genuinely interested in him and wanted to get to know him.

One evening, he went to a dance club called the Star Palace with one of his roommates, and across the room he noticed a petite young woman with strikingly good looks staring back at him. She wasn't hard to miss, being one of the few dark-haired people in the building besides Tony. He asked her to dance and mused while they slow danced. He realized he was at least a foot taller than she was. He wondered to himself whether he could ever be attracted to someone so tiny. But he and Alyssa hit it off right away. They spent the rest of the evening at the club talking and getting to know one another. Alyssa was of Italian and German ancestry, and a student at Ricks College, a private university of the LDS Church in Rexburg, Idaho, some 240 miles from Salt Lake City. As their relationship blossomed, aided by many long-distance telephone calls, Alyssa invited Tony to come for a weekend visit.

Tony made the four-hour drive to Rexburg during a brutally cold and harsh winter and brought along one of his college friends, who Alyssa had set up with one of her friends. The college was rigidly conservative, as were the rules of the apartments Alyssa lived in. No boys were allowed at any time, but Alyssa and her friend smuggled Tony and his buddy inside for a special home-cooked meal. In the middle of dinner, security showed up, forcing Tony and his friend to make a hasty retreat out of a back window some two stories up. The boys were overtaken by laughter as they hung on a windowsill, contemplating the drop. Tony went first, using his martial arts skills to roll once he hit the ground to absorb the shock, but his friend nearly broke his leg when he hit the hard-packed snow and ice below.

Tony and Alyssa's relationship was on-again-off-again over the next two years. They'd be together, have a disagreement over one thing or another, agree to date other people, then find themselves right back together again. That is, until they broke up yet again during a particularly harsh Utah winter before the end of the first semester of Tony's sophomore year, and right before he came down with a nasty case of mono. This time, he was sure it would be the end for the two of them. He'd been sick before but had experienced nothing like this. He recalled what he had gone through as a small child when he came down with one thing after another. He felt lucky to be alive, given that the child mortality rate was terribly high at that time.

He was too sick to go to school and had missed far too many classes over several weeks that semester, forcing him to fall further and further behind. He eventually decided that in his physical state, the smartest thing for him to do was to take a leave of absence and move back out west, where it was warmer, so he could better recuperate and get his mind right.

He bundled himself up as best as he could and, with a high fever, made his way to the campus administrative offices to begin the process of officially withdrawing from school. As soon as he got back home to the two-room apartment he shared with five roommates, he passed out on his bed and stayed there for what seemed like an eternity.

As his condition worsened, his roommates decided to notify his father and then took him to the school health center, where he was prescribed an antibiotic. It caused a severe allergic reaction and made him have an unusual experience of what he thought was the afterlife. He saw himself, his ancestors, and other spirits in an otherworldly realm. When his dad arrived, he found Tony quarantined in the corner of his room and delirious. With the help of some of his roommates, Tony's El Camino was quickly packed with his few belongings in no time. With his father in the driver's seat and Tony as the passenger, the two men began their drive out of Provo, Utah, to California. His dad and Helen were only too happy to make space for him in their two-room apartment. Once again, Tony's bed was someone else's couch.

Tony and his 1969 El Camino

A few months later, just as Tony began getting settled again, his dad received a promising job offer in San Diego that he couldn't pass up. Before he accepted the offer, Tony's dad told him the good—or not so good—news. "I've been offered a job with a company based in San Diego. I've been thinking, and I really believe that this would be a great opportunity for us to make a fresh start. San Diego's a wonderful place to live. We've found a nice apartment in the city of Santee next to El Cajon, and you can finally have your own bedroom again. Plus, it's right next to Grossmont Community College."

Eduardo kept telling Tony all about San Diego, painting a perfect picture of their next great adventure, just as he'd always done. Tony sat on the couch in the living room of their two-room apartment, listening to his dad and trying to imagine what it was going to be like. Tony's dad accepted the offer, and he and Helen soon moved into the new apartment in San Diego. Tony would follow after he finished his final exams.

Tony settled in quickly, began classes at Grossmont College, and took a job as a campus police officer. He also took additional courses taught by a lieutenant from the El Cajon Police Department that would give him the certifications he would need to apply to become a reserve officer.

Years later, Tony again encountered his teacher, who had risen to chief of police for El Cajon. Tony, at that time, was an FBI supervisory special agent managing an organized crime, drugs, gangs, and violent crimes squad in San Diego. He was attending a law memorial event as a guest speaker in San Diego, honoring officers who had died in the line of duty. His former teacher was also on the dais, and the two men took the opportunity to reconnect. Tony thanked the man for helping lay a foundation for his future work, and his mentor took great pride that one of his former students had done so well in their chosen profession.

Less than a year after settling down in their new lives in San Diego, Eduardo came home after work at the beginning of summer with some news that would have the family packing and heading back to Los Angeles County once again. The job that held so much promise was no more—the company was going out of business. Eduardo found himself looking for another job with no choice but to move in with Helen's parents. Unable to afford his own apartment, Tony found himself without a home and on the move again.

Eddie had worked very hard and had begun renting a small apartment in Downey, not far from Helen's parent's house, and was more than happy to offer his brother a place to stay. Once again, Tony found himself couch-surfing and tried hard not to be a burden on his brother or father. He scoured the classifieds every day, circling possible jobs he could take until school started again in the fall.

At the small kitchen table in his brother's cramped apartment, Tony heard a knock at the door. It was his father stopping by to say hi, which had become a regular occurrence. Tony kept munching on a bowl of granola while his dad nervously started talking about Alyssa and family and starting over. As Tony looked up from his cereal at his father, he squinted slightly as he tried to understand what his dad, who was now sheepishly chuckling, was trying to tell him. Just then, the door opened and in walked Alyssa, backlit by glowing morning sunshine that beamed into the room as she entered.

Tony needed a moment to process what he was seeing. Their last breakup had been hard on Tony, and he was still holding on to feelings of resentment; he was not as happy to see her as she was to see him. With his recent setbacks, the last thing on Tony's mind was rekindling a relationship with her. One wouldn't have known that by the excitement Alyssa displayed. As far as she was concerned, they had never parted ways.

Tony's father, who thought the world of Tony's presumptive future wife, had encouraged the surprise trip. Being a typical teenager, Tony hadn't kept his father apprised of the inner workings of his romantic relationships. Still, Eduardo's impressions of Alyssa were that she cared for Tony and made his son happy when they had first met. He knew that she came from a good family and had a strong moral foundation. He was confident that whatever had happened between them could be worked out.

Unbeknownst to Tony, Alyssa had taken it upon herself to arrange everything, including her flight and the taxi from the airport to Helen's family's home. Her unexpected arrival made for an awkward morning at first, although Tony eventually lightened up.

During the following week, Tony slowly opened up to the idea of giving their relationship one more try. After she asked, he began entertaining the idea of going to Las Vegas with her for the summer. Tony, always up for an adventure, knew Alyssa had a huge family there, and her father's company had a couple of summer job openings Tony would be perfect for. Alyssa's grandmother had a spare bedroom for Tony to stay in. The more he thought about it, the better it sounded to him. Besides, the two main issues Tony had been diligently trying to find a solution to—a job and a place to live—could be resolved in one fell swoop. Eduardo strongly suggested that he go with her.

Tony loved spending time with Alyssa's family. Her mother was a very kind and generous woman, whom the entire family adored. She doted on each family member and made the most delicious food Tony had tasted in quite some time. Alyssa's parent's home was quiet during the day and bustling with cousins, aunts, uncles, and grandparents every night. Children's laughter could be heard from each room, with loud conversations about everything going on at the same time. Tony began to enjoy this animated and loving environment that felt so much like the home he grew up in. As he grew closer and closer to the family, he felt as though he had finally found a place where he fit in. He took his new role as Uncle Tony to the kids seriously. He loved playing silly games with them and was taken by how loving Alyssa's mother was toward the entire family and now toward him as well. The more time Tony spent with the family, the more the idea of Tony and Alyssa getting married was brought up. Her family thought highly of Tony and encouraged the young couple to make it official and get married.

The issues that had previously plagued their relationship were not ever discussed or resolved. Instead, they lay below the surface of the loud chatter of her parents' home, much like pebbles hidden under a rug. Those small pebbles struck a nerve with Tony at unexpected times in random conversations. Determined to ignore those feelings, Tony rationalized with himself that he would simply rope off the place in his heart Alyssa had broken, making it no longer accessible to her. Being a young man and not very experienced in matters of the heart, Tony underestimated the long-term effects of old wounds. Knowing that the apple doesn't fall far from the tree, he reasoned that Alyssa was a good person and would be a good mother. He imagined a future with a large home filled with family, children, food, and laughter. He had become quite attached to her family. Her father was self-made, and Tony was determined to be able to one day say the same thing of himself.

After much persuasion by both eager families, Tony and Alyssa decided to get married in a small ceremony in a Mormon temple in St. George, Utah, attended by a few close friends and family. Although he appreciated the job her father had given him, Tony remained focused on finishing his education, knowing it was one of the key factors he had always been told was part of the path to success. Alyssa was supportive of this, and they worked together to map it out. They planned to save enough money to return to Utah so Tony could graduate.

CHAPTER 13

Newlyweds

THE NEWLYWEDS ARRIVED BACK IN UTAH WITH JUST ENOUGH money to rent a small apartment in Provo and furnish it with whatever they could find. Alyssa's father, who had not been entirely supportive of the marriage because of their young age, made it clear that he was not going to offer any financial aid. Tony realized that the responsibility of supporting his wife was squarely on his shoulders and that if he were to climb the economic ladder, he would need to finish his college education first. Starting a family could only come after graduation and after he got a stable job, so he threw himself into his studies and had little time for anything else except a job with the campus police, one that he thoroughly enjoyed.

Tony drove an old Volkswagen with no air-conditioning and a front driver's seat that wouldn't stay bolted down, a constant nuisance if not a safety issue. The apartment they could afford was a converted bomb shelter beneath a single-family home that had been renovated. It was adequate except for an exposed drainpipe that ran directly above their bed. They would hear a surge from the old lead pipe every time a toilet was flushed.

Tony began making a standing joke of it and would launch into his own rendition of Robin Leach, delivering one of his famous monologues from *The Lifestyles of the Rich and Famous*. "And it's Robin Leach. I circle the globe seeking stories that America will never stop talking about," he'd say with great exuberance. "Tonight's Cinderella story features Alyssa Arismendi, who went from schoolgirl to a loving wife. This lucky woman found the glass slipper and now lives the lifestyle she deserves, one of champagne wishes and caviar dreams!"

If there was any stress in their relationship, it was over money. There was never enough to make ends meet. Alyssa did not have much work experience, never having needed to work as a student. She got a job at a Pizza Hut (which lasted but one day) but didn't find a steady job until she got on with a home goods company, Leather Oak and Brass, and began to do very well, making herself indispensable to the small company.

Tony and his mom reunite in California

The realities of day-to-day life and its struggles soon caught up with them. Tony was devoting all of his time and attention to school and work, and although Alyssa was contributing, it was a constant battle for them to pay their bills. It didn't help that he was committed to sending fifty dollars a month to Venezuela to assist his mother, who was suffering from the rising economic instability there and having a hard time making it on her own as a single woman. Her father had passed away, and with him went the financial aid he had provided her. The money Tony sent only added to the strain he and Alyssa had on their finances every month. The burden of rent, tuition, books, food, transportation, and the rest of their expenses seemed insurmountable. Tony began to seriously think about quitting school. He didn't care if he had to drive a truck—he felt his first priority was to provide for his wife and lessen any hardship on her.

Tony preferred to study on campus and would always try to sit in the same cubicle in a corner on the fourth floor of the Harold B. Lee Library. One evening, he found himself unable to concentrate as he'd all but resigned that he would have to quit school. Instead of the reading he was to be doing for his class, he began another all-too-familiar conversation with himself. His mind was racing as he went over what he'd have to do to take a formal leave of absence and find a full-time job. In the back of his mind was the nagging concern that once he made this decision, he might never return to finish his degree. But he had run the numbers so many times in his mind that he was sure there was no way out other than to quit.

Then something caught his eye. Within arm's reach sat an oversized book bound in a light blue cover. He reached for it, then saw the title on its spine. It read *The Revolution of South America, 1808–1833*. He plopped it onto his desk and flipped it open. He studied the page he'd opened to in amazement, startled to see a beautiful portrait of Juan Bautista Arismendi in full dress uniform. He quickly read the accompanying story that told of his great-great-great-grandfather's exploits in South America's war of independence. Every hair on his body stood on end as he began to process what was happening. He'd been studying at the same spot for over two years right next to that book. And on the day he'd decided to quit school and rethink his life, he randomly pulled out his great-great-great-grandfather's story.

Tony knew this was much more than a coincidence. It was as if his ancestors were not so subtly interacting with him to encourage him when he needed it most. His mind raced as he recounted the trials and tribulations that General Arismendi and Luisa Cáceres de Arismendi had endured, which were inextricably connected to Tony being alive in the first place. What if General Arismendi had quit, he wondered? What if he had taken off his uniform and ran when times got tough? He would've never been in a position to reunite with his wife Luisa after she escaped from Spain, and the family history would never have evolved the way it had.

As though jolted from another dimension, Tony realized that if General Arismendi and Luisa Cáceres de Arismendi could refuse to give up even after everything they went through, then surely Tony could figure out a way to stay in school and not give up on his educational goals. The obstacles facing his ancestors were far more serious, compelling, and of an entirely different nature than what Tony was facing now. Reflecting on this put things into perspective for him, and he realized his current predicament was a far cry from the life-or-death dilemma they had faced and overcome. And besides, he thought, quitting just wasn't in the family genes!

Tony rushed to the nearest pay phone and called Alyssa at home. She was going to be picking him up that evening, but he asked her to come early so he could show her something important. When she met him at the library, Tony showed her the book and excitedly recounted what had just happened. Certain it was a sign from a higher power, he told Alyssa that he wanted to stay in school and try to work through their predicament, one way or another. If he had to take on another job and forgo sleep, he would do whatever it took, and they would make it somehow.

So Tony kept his nose to the grindstone and managed to keep up with his studies and his part-time police work. As the months passed and their finances stabilized, he became more and more confident that he'd find a lucrative job.

One of his fellow campus police officers was the son of a retired FBI agent, who began talking to Tony about the Bureau. Tony had met the older man, who developed an interest in him. Little by little, the man continued to water the seed that had been planted years ago in Tony's mind.

While his long-term dream of becoming an FBI agent was growing, he achieved an incredible milestone in his life—and one required to become an FBI agent—he was granted US citizenship. One of the happiest moments in his life.

CHAPTER 14

Looking to the Stars for Guidance

Tony had known about astrology for some time and had treated it as a complement to other aspects of the spiritual journey he was on. He'd read book after book on this ancient system of knowledge and found himself devoting much of his free time to learning more. As his interest grew, he started doing charts for his friends and often blew them away with the accuracy of his readings.

"How in the heck did you know that about me?" they'd ask.

"It's right there in your chart!" he'd reply.

His friends would shake their heads in disbelief, not willing at first to accept that Tony could be so accurate with personal insight about their lives that they hadn't revealed to him.

When he first started doing readings, he managed to surprise even himself when he'd chart a person's time and place of birth and chart the relative positions of planets and stars. Armed with this information, he made observations by tuning into them on a deeper level and offered an interpretation that was both accurate and beneficial to them. He didn't know exactly how he was able to do this at first; it simply seemed that impressions would just come to him that he enjoyed passing along to help them and encourage his friends.

More than once, friends of his who knew little about astrology were mystified by the reading they'd just gotten. They would want Tony to give them an explanation of how he'd known so much about them. Since he loved the subject and was always willing to talk about it, he'd tell them that casting a person's astrological chart starts with obtaining information about their birth: date, time, and precise geographical location. The study and application of astrology presuppose that the alignment of the sun, moon, and planets within our solar system will collectively create an "energy grid" that will imprint on a person during the moment they are born. These are known as natal charts.

All masses exert a gravitational pull or influence on other masses. Our sun exerts its gravitational force on the planets within the solar system, keeping them in balance and orbit. The planets also exert their own force in return. The Earth keeps the moon within its orbit, and the moon's gravitational forces pull on the Earth, most easily demonstrated by the movement of ocean tides. Although the other planets are distant, they too exert a certain gravitational force upon the Earth and its inhabitants.

The study of astrology began in ancient Sumer and was refined by the Babylonians. As the Earth, moon, and planets proceed through their orbits around the sun, the astrologers noted different patterns of their orbits. Astrologers saw these patterns were connected to events on Earth and their impact on people. These observations also identified chief characteristics of the sun, moon, and planets, and were refined over thousands of years to provide the basis for how astrological charts are interpreted.

Astrologers maintain that the interpretation of an individual's chart can reveal past experiences, past lives, strength of character, dominant traits, and past traumas. The concentration of planets in a zodiacal house may also indicate specific energy and purpose. How the planets will be moving in comparison to a person's natal chart can also provide insight into upcoming events or challenges and changes one may face. These are called transit charts and are regularly used to determine the timing of meetings, the formation of companies, the execution of contracts, or times to avoid starting new ventures, such as during Mercury retrograde, when these types of things often get thrown off course. US president Ronald Reagan routinely used the services of an astrologer, Joan Quigley, to make crucial decisions while in office. He timed such things as working with Mikhail Gorbachev or when to take meetings, summits, and even his inauguration so that an endeavor would be most likely to succeed.

The interpretation of astrological charts took Tony many years to master. Decades of experience have revealed that other factors, such as a person's culture and where they were raised, have an effect on the final form of an astrological chart. Tony also found that his innate sense of intuition came into play when interpreting a person's chart. This intuition, combined with his other knowledge and experiences, led Tony to trust astrology more and more, and led to many startling responses from friends, family members, and others who asked him to do their chart.

In response to the inevitable from a shocked client, he would say, "Well, it's right there in your chart!" And he would begin to explain how this planet was conjoined with that planet and what was rising, what was descending, and what was transitioning. He found he became quite adept at it, and to this day, family, friends, and clients seek him out for his observations and advice.

Tony would find later in his law enforcement career that he could use astrology to help him get into the mindset of his adversaries. During his time in the FBI, in many of the cases he worked, astrology helped in determining a target's next move. He kept it quiet to avoid having to explain his use of this unconventional tool to his colleagues, but Tony was devoted to the old adage, "know your enemy."

CHAPTER 15

Becoming a Father

TONY CONTINUED TO WORK HARD, AS HE KNEW THAT THROUGH determination and the guidance he had received from both his father and grandfather, the sky was the limit. He was in love with life and with the prospect of growing a family, and it didn't take long for Alyssa to become pregnant.

Tony called her from a pay phone adjacent to a bustling quad on the BYU campus after her doctor's appointment one afternoon. As the phone rang in his home, he studied the hundreds of students, all scurrying in different directions like ants on a hill as they rushed to their next classes. Tears welled in his eyes when Alyssa shared with him her suspicion had been confirmed—they were expecting a baby. Tony pinched himself to make sure he was not dreaming. He was overwhelmed, thinking about how fortunate he was that he had managed to come to the greatest country in the world. One that accepted those from other countries, where there were opportunities for anyone willing to work hard, and where he had mastered a new language. He had finished high school and was about to finish college with good grades, despite the absence of help from his family. He had found a beautiful wife, and now he was going to become a father, the highest calling he had ever imagined. As he walked away from the phone booth, he knew his feet were making contact with the cobblestone courtyard beneath him, yet he felt like he was walking on air.

It was a great feeling he would experience yet again when he left the hospital after cutting the umbilical cord of his newborn son, whom he and Alyssa named Anthony.

Little Anthony was a beautiful baby. He had a shock of dirty blond hair with beautiful green eyes. And unlike a lot of newborns whose faces are squished and contorted in the birthing process, Anthony by all measures had a very handsome little face from day one. Tony could not be prouder, even as he was somewhat perplexed and overwhelmed. As he held his first son in his arms, it fully sank in that he was now responsible for another human being. Even though he had been around younger siblings and cousins, he quickly realized his son didn't come with an owner's manual. Tony would have to learn on the job. He had taken classes in infant CPR and safety, and began reading just about every book he found on the care and feeding of newborns.

Alyssa received all the help and support she needed from her large and committed family, her mother staying with them for a couple of weeks after Anthony's birth to give her a hand with the baby. When Tony's college graduation day arrived, both families came to celebrate. At a party after the commencement, Tony beamed and posed for picture after picture, holding little Anthony in one arm and his diploma in business management in the other.

CHAPTER 16

Las Vegas

THE HAPPY COUPLE SOON MOVED TO LAS VEGAS SO ALYSSA COULD be closer to her family. Tony did not seek, nor would he have accepted, any help from Alyssa's father. He wasn't interested in working in their family construction business and went about diligently distributing his résumé all over town. It didn't take long for him to land a position as an accountant with a subsidiary of the Circus Circus Casino. Tony soon discovered that he was not cut out to be a bean counter, but the position was at least within his area of expertise. He reasoned it would be a positive stepping stone to something else where he could utilize his business degree and begin to build a solid résumé. He held on to the job just long enough to find something else that would bring home the bacon.

The truth of the matter was Tony had no problem with the challenge. He had confidence that he would be able to provide for his family and give his wife the lifestyle she was used to. He assured Alyssa that their sacrifices were temporary, but he also knew she was having a harder time of it than he was. Tony continued to submit applications for any position available.

It was not a vibrant job market at the time, but this didn't stop him from turning over every rock. It was at this time that Tony took a step that had been a long time in the making. He drove to the Federal building on South Las Vegas Boulevard and walked into an FBI field office. He met an agent by the name of Don Kelso, who was in charge of recruiting. Don was a seasoned FBI agent in the mold of the prototypical J. Edgar Hoover–era G-man. Don was dressed impeccably in a tailored suit and a starched button-down dress shirt, his tie knotted in a perfect Windsor, with not a hair out of place atop his head. He exuded confidence, and Tony was duly impressed. Tony found himself meeting someone who could have starred in his favorite childhood television program back in Venezuela.

After a long first conversation, Don gave Tony some tests, including a written Spanish test, and made it a point to tell Tony that the FBI was very interested in recruits who spoke fluent Spanish. Tony had passed the sniff test and began building a relationship with Don, who took a liking to him and began encouraging him along the way. Don also made Tony well aware of the reality that getting into the FBI and becoming an agent was not going to be easy, and it wasn't going to be quick.

He escorted Tony out of the building that day. When Don noticed Tony checking out other governmental agencies that had signs out for qualified recruits they passed, Don grabbed his shoulder and ushered him right past the signs and job board.

Tony glanced back at the Drug Enforcement Agency (DEA) office, and Don told him, "You don't want to work for them, you'll only work drugs." When they passed the ATF office, Don said, "Alcohol, tobacco, and firearms? That could get real boring, real quick." And of the CIA, Don said, "You go to work for them, and you'll never really know who your friends are." He paused for effect. "But you go to work for us, and you'll work everything there is, and you'll get to move around every few years. You'll never be bored. I guarantee you that. Everyone will know you're a member of the finest law enforcement agency in the world. You won't wind up behind some desk in some God-forsaken foreign country. And you'll start as a GS-10, not a seven like those guys. That's a nice chunk of money."

Tony liked what Don was selling. He knew that he was buying, even as he was made acutely aware that getting accepted into the Academy was far from a slam dunk.

Tony had become friends with an older couple, Richard and Ginger Beers, who lived in the apartment next door. Richard was a retired Army colonel who had served in Korea, then Vietnam. Displayed on the wall of Richard's nicely furnished den was an assortment of memorabilia he had gathered over his illustrious career. Tony was drawn to a framed letter of commendation that then Major Beers had received from President Nixon in 1970 for his heroic actions in a battle in Vietnam.

Colonel Richard Beers was indeed highly decorated during his military career, having accumulated many honors and citations, including the Bronze Star and the Silver Star, badges that Tony had only heard about but had never seen before in person. Richard had earned them all, including the Purple Heart and the Combat Infantryman's Badge, given to officers below the rank of colonel who personally fought in ground war combat. The colonel's medals were encased in crafted wooden boxes that Richard kept on a coffee table.

Unfortunately, the colonel also wore an additional badge that many Vietnam vets shared: the side effects of Agent Orange exposure. The defoliant chemical was used extensively to deprive guerrillas of food and concealment and to clear sensitive areas, such as base perimeters. As with many veterans exposed to the chemical, Colonel Beers had developed leukemia. At the point when Tony met Richard, the colonel's health was rapidly deteriorating, and he was beginning to want to talk with Tony more and more, telling him things he had never told another living soul. Richard treated Tony like a son, and they quickly bonded.

Baby Anthony and Colonel Richard Beers

Tony would sit with him for hours and talk about all things military, particularly Richard's war experiences. He confided in Tony his stories of combat—the heartbreak and the horror of it—but what stayed with Tony more than those images was how the colonel strove to do what was right, always adhering to a strict code of honor. The retired officer had tried to weigh all of his decisions against something honest, true, and good that emanated from deep within his soul. Colonel Beers managed to keep his spirit true while giving his all to his country, his men, and his family.

Tony developed the utmost respect for Richard for his selfless service and considered the man to be a true hero—one of many Tony regarded as unsung heroes who answered their calling, fulfilled their duty, and toiled tirelessly, not needing or seeking the reward of notoriety. Richard had worn the uniform and had been willing to die in support of his convictions. It evoked in Tony a pride in the ethos of the universal soldier and a deep and abiding veneration for that indomitable spirit that resides in all who choose to walk the warrior's path.

Tony's application process to the FBI continued. He took required tests and passed them all. It would still take some time to be admitted to an FBI Academy training class, but he began to look toward the FBI as a career, knowing full well it would be a difficult job to balance with marriage and a baby son. He didn't know if the FBI would afford a comfortable lifestyle for his growing family, but he knew there would be plenty of opportunities and room for advancement within the Bureau. He also knew that what had swayed him inexorably toward making that decision was the influence Colonel Beers had on him. The way the Colonel had served his country, the kind of man he was, inspired Tony to continue the application process toward reaching his lifelong goal of joining the FBI.

But in the meantime, Tony still had to meet his financial responsibilities. He had a friend who owned a service station that was losing money due to improper management. The friend asked Tony for help, and in little time, Tony was able to turn the business around and was compensated with a percentage of profits. He utilized this income to get into the vending machine business. Tony leased machines and quickly realized that a great location was more important than the machine or the product. Using a lot of grit and determination, combined with his formidable sales skills, Tony managed to place a number of machines in good locations, including some hotels and casinos. He also had gotten a real estate license, began working on a broker's license, and began planning a third venture with a laundromat business.

Tony always recalled the valuable encouragement his grandfather instilled in him to always believe in yourself. Tony's unfailing self-confidence allowed him to create opportunities where others would have backed down. When he started his vending machine business, Tony managed to secure a contract to have soda vending machines placed at hotels and various businesses. But Tony didn't yet own a single machine, nor had he ever run a vending machine company. He set out on this enterprise on a whim, utilizing another trait he had developed—never take no for an answer.

For example, Tony had once snuck into a hotel manager's office after having been denied an appointment. When Tony cornered the executive a second time, the exasperated man heard him out, and Tony's persistence awarded him the contract for the entire hotel. Tony had two weeks to have the existing machines removed and his machines installed. With the contract firmly in hand, Tony endeavored to schedule some face time with a soda distributor. When he again sought out the person in charge, he got a similarly chilly reception. But with a hotel contract in hand and the same determination he had shown before, they came to an agreement to place machines in the hotel.

He had created something out of nothing with sheer determination and an abiding belief in himself. He would revisit this story many times in the future as a reminder to himself and others he later mentored about the power of persistence and confidence. Knowing that anything can be accomplished, even when it isn't clear exactly how, is an extremely powerful tool.

Tony continued to market himself relentlessly. He had a goal of sending out twenty-five résumés a day and always met it. One caught the eye of a human resources manager at Dillard's, the department store chain that had a store in Las Vegas, and that led to Tony's initial interview. Although he had no retail experience, Tony kept getting called back for more interviews and eventually was flown to Phoenix, where he had a meeting with one of the company's presidents, a no-nonsense New Yorker.

"So, what do you do, kid?" the executive asked abruptly.

"Well, I'm a real estate agent, have a vending machine business, and I also manage some businesses for a few people."

"And you just graduated from college?"

"Yes, sir. With a BS in business administration. And I'm getting ready to start another company."

"And in your free time you…"

"I'm sorry, sir, there is no free time. I'm working seven days a week, and I wish I could do eight."

"At least you know what it takes to get ahead."

"I hope so, sir."

"That's what I did when I was your age. It ain't about luck, kid. As that golfer says, the harder you work, the luckier you get." The executive picked up Tony's application and quickly scanned it. "I see you're married? And one child?"

"Yes, sir."

"That will keep you focused and away from too much of the high life—if you know what I mean."

Tony nodded. "I've never had that luxury, sir. No time for that with my studies and work."

"That's great, Tony. A lot of young people now, that's all they think about. They don't realize the importance of deferred gratification. They're out at the discos drinking and carrying on, and thinking they can do justice to their careers at the same time." He leaned in closer to Tony. "That's why most of the young people start with us on the floor, and it can take years before they get all of that out of their system and they make manager level." The man paused a long moment and took Tony's measure again. "So why do you want to work for us?"

"I want to learn retail from the bottom up, apply myself, and take care of my family."

"I learned two things from my father that he thought were real important. Knowledge is power, and work hard to take care of your family. Which one do you think is more important?"

Tony did not hesitate. "If one is educated to the best of one's ability, then I'd say that would necessarily lead to working smarter, and that would lead to being more easily able to take care of one's family," he said thoughtfully, being sure to look the man directly in the eye.

"Why do you think you'd make a good manager?"

"It's part of my background, sir. Both sides of my family in Venezuela were involved in owning and running various businesses. My family also has a long history in the military, and I hope some of their leadership qualities have rubbed off on me. I think they have. I believe I understand psychology and what motivates people, and how to get the best out of them. I'm also confident in my ability to analyze a situation, come up with a smart plan of action, and execute by delegation and working with other people."

"How do you get the best out of people, do you think?"

"By showing respect and leading by example, sir."

The manager liked what he heard. He asked, "So what do you know about Dillard's?"

Tony was ready for him, as he had gone to the library and studied their prospectus before the meeting. "Well, I know your store in Las Vegas has approximately 26,000 square feet, with about 150 employees. This one store generated a substantial amount in revenue last year, and your asset to debt ratio is very good. The state of the aggregate market value of your corporate voting stock is phenomenal and getting stronger. You're one of the top retailers in the country, and I would very much appreciate the opportunity to work for you."

The man was clearly impressed. "Most of our managers don't even know this information. I'll tell you what, kid. How about we make you an offer? We have a management program."

Tony sat up straighter in his chair, trying not to show too much emotion.

"We can start you off at $27,000 a year."

Tony slumped but quickly caught himself and cleared his throat. "Well, last year I did well and made more than that on my own." Tony paused, searching for the words. "With all due respect, I couldn't afford to work for you at that salary. I appreciate your meeting with me, but I can't accept your offer."

The executive sat back in his chair and leaned into his hands, clasped behind his head, the wheels turning in his head as he gazed into the ceiling, looking at nothing in particular.

"Okay. I'll tell you what I'm going to do. And we're both going to take a lot of heat for this, but I think you can handle it, and hey, I'm the boss. You're going to be managing people older than you who have taken ten to fifteen years to rise into management, and there's bound to be a lot of resentment. But I'm going to start you as assistant store manager in Las Vegas. As you are aware, it's one of four top stores but has fallen off recently. I'll have HR contact you about your compensation package. I'm sure it will make you happy. Welcome aboard, son."

The men shook hands as Tony responded with a sincere "Thank you."

As he walked out of the meeting that day, he realized that he was happy working his little businesses and had been doing well. Still, he also understood the opportunity now before him. He had planned to continue the application process with the FBI while he worked at Dillard's, hoping to learn how the big boys did it, even if it meant that he would have to cut back on his entrepreneurial businesses. He knew this would give him a better idea of the bigger picture in business, and then later, he could go off again and do his own thing.

CHAPTER 17

Undercover Boss

THE DILLARD'S STORE MANAGER, LISA MALKOVICH, FELT threatened by Tony's presence. And she was sure she was justified in feeling that way. Who was this young guy who came along without retail experience, or without much job experience for that matter, and thought he could run a store like this one? Tony knew she secretly hoped that he would fail. He set about trying to win her over, a task that would prove time consuming and difficult, if not impossible. But he first turned his attention to learning the business from the bottom up.

Tony started as a shipping clerk in the warehouse and then rotated from position to position, from the credit department to the sales floor. His undercover work lasted but a few weeks, until a profile on him was published in their store newsletter and his coworkers were surprised to see that Tony was, in reality, their boss. But he had learned a great deal by listening to them as he compiled a manual with a page in it for each employee with their photograph affixed to the top. He memorized their names and a little something about them, so when he engaged with them, he could always ask them about their families or about how they were doing on a more personal level. Tony found that going the extra mile in the trenches, working alongside people in different departments, went a long way toward gaining acceptance—and the loyalty of the two-hundred-plus people who worked at Dillard's.

When they tried to address him as Mr. Arismendi, Tony quickly insisted on being called Tony. "Mr. Arismendi is my dad," he would say. "Just call me Tony."

Tony began to love his new job, finding it to be a tremendous learning experience. He had an open-door policy, and anyone could come into his office and receive his undivided attention. He taped all the soap operas and let them play on a loop in the break room. He organized team-building activities and emphasized cohesiveness among the employees, feeling more like a captain on a cruise ship or a mayor of a little town than a supervisor.

Tony learned to make many off-the-cuff decisions, quickly figuring out what would work and what wouldn't. "Put those jeans over here! Move that display over there!" he'd say to a department manager. Or he'd ask them for their input and not hesitate to give something new a try. The store had a phenomenal run, and the senior management of the company was delighted.

William Dillard, the patriarch of the Dillard family, visited the store and congratulated Lisa and Tony on one of the most profitable years the store had ever had. He autographed a copy of his biography for Tony and personally presented it to him.

A critical prerequisite to the job that Tony was grateful for was that he learned men's fashion from the inside out, being required to sport a certain look in his position at Dillard's. In the process, he amassed an enviable collection of Armani suits and jackets, custom shirts and silk ties, and high-quality shoes, all items that would prove useful in his work to come with the FBI. Knowing style and how to put together outfits becoming of a midlevel drug lord went a long way when Tony's new job required him to con the cons on behalf of the FBI.

At the same time Tony was distinguishing himself at Dillard's, his application to the FBI made its way through the slow and methodical process typical of government. He would be called in for occasional new rounds of testing and, at one point, was informed he was competing against 1,200 other people for the same job. At any given time, the FBI has over 100,000 applications on file. Of those, only roughly 4 percent are accepted. Despite those long odds, he continued with the process. He held out hope that his background and fluency in Spanish would help his application—he knew the Bureau was especially interested in Black people, Hispanic people, and women because, at that time, the landscape of America was changing, and the FBI intended to keep up with it.

As the application process for the Bureau dragged on, Tony found he was becoming more and more content with the thought of keeping his new position at Dillard's. Deep in his heart, he knew he had a private-sector mentality—he thought outside of the box. He feared that in government, one had to learn to "go along to get along," and Tony knew that would be difficult for him. His dream of becoming an FBI agent was beginning to lose its luster as the FBI's schedule did not mesh with what was happening in Tony's rocketing business career. He began to think more and more about staying the course on his now-successful path in the business world.

One evening, Tony received word from the FBI recruiter, Don, who called him to tell him he was doing great in the application process. "I wanted to let you know that everything is good."

Tony hesitated, and an uncomfortable silence hung in the air as he collected his thoughts. "Well, Don, I've been doing a lot of thinking lately, and things are going so well at the store, I really don't know if I still want to do this."

"Hey, you're almost at the finish line. Just hang in there a bit more with me on this, will you? We are almost done. There's only one thing left to do."

"What's that?"

"We just need to interview your employer," Don said.

Tony's wheels began to turn. "And what happens if I don't get the job with the Bureau, and now Dillard's knows I've applied?"

Don did not have a compelling answer for that and spent the better part of the next hour trying to talk Tony into continuing with the application process. By the end of the conversation, Tony told him that he was inclined to continue but wanted to sleep on it. They agreed that Tony would call him in the morning with his decision about whether he would allow the FBI to call Dillard's but insisted upon calling the company's president himself. It was a tough decision that Tony finally made, concluding that fulfilling a lifetime ambition was more important than immediate success in business.

The next morning, he reached out to the executive at Dillard's headquarters in Arkansas. "Well, I have some good news, and I have some bad news," Tony told his mentor. "The good news is our numbers are way up over last month, and we're doing unbelievably well. The bad news is I might have to leave."

"You're being recruited by Saks Fifth Avenue...I knew that was going to happen!"

"Well, yes. They did call me to be general manager of one of their stores in New York."

"Those bastards!"

"So did Neiman Marcus."

"What did they offer? We can match it. Hell, we'll better it! You're not going to go with them, are you?"

"No."

"That's great, son. You know you've got a home here with us."

"Well, I told both of them I wasn't interested." Tony took a moment to clear his throat, then said, "Sir, actually...I'm going to become an FBI agent."

The man laughed without thinking. "An FBI agent?! This is a joke, right?"

"No. I'm serious."

"So what are you going to do? Are you going to carry a gun?"

"Yes, sir. That comes with the job."

Tony's mentor was a man feared within the company as a hard-nosed executive, but he sensed Tony's commitment and had no question about his abilities. The executive finally got the message that Tony was definitely leaving and definitely going into the FBI. The man's affinity for his protégé won out, and the man gave him his blessing and agreed to meet with the FBI on Tony's behalf.

"You're a dyed-in-the-wool executive. I can't imagine you chasing bad guys down back alleys. I had big plans for you, son. But if that's what you want to do, I wish you well..."

Tony gave his formal notice and began the process of saying goodbye to his colleagues and staff, who threw a huge going-away party for him. The store manager Lisa Malkovich happily attended, relieved that the threat to her standing in the company was no more.

CHAPTER 18

When Opportunity Meets Preparation

BEFORE THE FBI INTERVIEWED TONY'S SOON-TO-BE EX-BOSS from Dillard's, they sat down with Alyssa. She had mixed feelings about Tony's career choice but knew it was Tony's dream, and she deferred to her husband. Alyssa recognized that Tony was a warrior at the core of his soul, and his lifelong dream was indelibly imprinted upon his being. She understood his inner calling would prove much stronger than his desire for success in business or the family's need for financial gain, for that matter. She also knew from experience that no one could tell Tony what to do or not do, including her. Once he set his mind on something, he was determined to make it happen, and attempting to get in the way would not do well for their relationship.

In her interview with the FBI, Alyssa let it be known that she was supportive but did not hold back that she was very concerned about the dangers he would encounter.

Tony began preparing himself by reading anything he could get his hands on about the FBI. He rented videos of every FBI movie ever made to watch in his spare time. The movie *Feds* had just come out. It was a comedy about two women newly admitted to the FBI Academy, where they learned about guns and crime and all else new recruits are exposed to. One of the women is a great student while the other excels in physical training, and they learn to help one another. Tony went to see the movie in a theater and soaked up all the film had to offer about FBI training, even as it presented the Academy in a comedic vein. He was later surprised to learn how accurate the film was in terms of the kinds of things he was to encounter at Quantico.

Another hugely successful film, *Mississippi Burning*, was released in 1989, and the hard-driving, realistic drama captivated him. He particularly liked Gene Hackman's spot-on portrayal of Agent Rupert Anderson, who was someone who could think out of the box and was not afraid to venture into those gray areas that often lead to solving a crime or closing a case. It was just such thinking that would greatly influence Tony's later successful work within the Bureau.

Tony also found James Stewart's interpretation of John Michael "Chip" Hardesty's character in the 1959 classic *The FBI Story* very compelling. Set in a telling of the history of the Bureau was one of the greatest actors of all time portraying a homespun, unassuming hero who puts his commitment to justice above all else, including his family, and who wins in the end. James Stewart's character was indeed just the kind of agent Tony would aspire to become.

At first, Tony's dad had mixed feelings about his decision. "Do you really want to do this?" his father asked.

"Yeah, Dad. It's what I want to do. And I got in on my own—no special favors, no family connections. I would've hoped you'd be proud of that."

"Well, sure, of course I am. But I worry about you, that's all. It's what parents do. You're talking about an extremely dangerous job. I don't want you to get yourself killed."

"Did you know that farmers, truck drivers, or even traveling salesmen are more likely to be killed on the job than law enforcement officers?"

"Statistics can say whatever you want them to say, son. Let's put it this way. If you told me you wanted to be a farmer, I'd feel a whole lot better, that's for sure. I think you'd be a whole lot less likely to be run over by a tractor than ambushed by some bad guy."

"Please don't worry about me, Dad. This is something I have to do. I'm going to be fine."

Even though Tony possessed the mindset of invincibility that comes with youth, the conversation with his father conjured images of what he'd been reading or seeing in the movies he'd been cramming into his head. He had just finished the book, *Donnie Brasco: My Undercover Life in the Mafia*, FBI Agent Joseph Pistone's harrowing account of his undercover work against the Mafia. The thought of living the life of an undercover agent and the danger that involved had become all too real in Tony's mind. In the end, the warrior in him won out. He held steadfast to his plan of action, despite being aware of how tough and dangerous the job could be and that he'd be putting his life on the line, as is the case for anyone who chooses to serve in law enforcement or the military. He also knew this job wouldn't be like fighting in a war zone on some battlefield, where bombs and bullets course through the air. It would be situations where people get killed or injured on the job doing very different types of dangerous things while interacting with a very different kind of dangerous people.

In federal law enforcement in the 1980s, the main battleground was the war on drugs, and Tony knew he would probably find himself in that arena. The famous Miami shoot-out where under-armed FBI agents lost their lives against the superior firepower of some very nasty bad guys had just occurred and was on everyone's mind. FBI agents had been involved in other shootings all over the country as well. Tony made a deal with himself that he would face whatever came up head-on and continue to hone his skills at "flipping the switch" for his protection and survival, to be able to instantly put himself in combat mode, a skill that would prove beneficial on many occasions to come.

Armed with a conditional letter of appointment to the FBI after giving up his job with Dillard's but not yet officially hired by the FBI, Tony had one more hurdle to clear before he would be able to start his official FBI training. There was a physical test he had to pass. He had already passed a preliminary test and now had to prove he could do it again while timed, and his repetitions counted under the watchful eye of his recruiter. Tony had managed to keep himself in top shape and wasn't too worried about passing, for the individual tests in and of themselves weren't that hard. It was that they had to be done in quick succession, so it was like a mini triathlon.

New male recruits had to do at least thirty-eight sit-ups in one minute, thirty push-ups in one minute, and their maximum number of pull-ups in one minute. Recruits had to run a 300-meter sprint in under 52.4 seconds, then complete a mile and a half run under twelve minutes and twenty-four seconds. They had few minutes between exercises for recovery. Recruits who failed the official test sometimes washed out. The reason being that if one can't perform to a minimum level, they would never survive the rigorous boot camp–like training ahead at the FBI Academy for everyone who passed the application process. It was better that those who couldn't perform the physical tests be weeded out before further investment in them was made.

Tony had been working on the test and had passed it on his own many times. Still, on the day Don had scheduled his official test, he was coming down with a bad case of the flu, undoubtedly passed along to him by his young child, who, like most toddlers, seemed to catch nearly every communicable illness that came his way.

Tony had severe chills and a fever. His muscles ached, and his bones felt like anchors pulling him down. He had nausea and dizziness, yet refused to cancel or postpone the test. He didn't know if he would get a second chance, and he never wanted to have to say, "You know, I once had a chance to join the FBI, but I got sick before my major physical test and didn't make it…"

He also knew that even if his test could be rescheduled, that would mean a delay, and he was already stressed enough. He had bills to pay and a family to support, and was anxious to begin his FBI training in the next Academy class so that he would officially be put on the payroll. Most importantly, he was not about to start his FBI career by asking for special consideration.

After some over-the-counter medication for his flu and fever, he met Don at Valley High School in Las Vegas, as planned. Tony sat in his car for a long time, trying to compose himself while preparing to be bright and chipper for Don when he showed up. Tony knew that, despite the strength of their relationship, Don was not going to cut him any slack.

As Don's car pulled up beside his in the parking lot, Tony thought, *Well, here we go!*

"Tony, my man. How are you?" Don inquired brightly.

"Great, Don. Just great."

"You ready to go? Don asked as he looked his charge over. "Sure, you are. You're going to knock this thing out of the park!"

"Yes, sir!"

Tony started one test and then another, all the while telling himself that he was going to do well. He was going to pass the exam or die trying. Somehow he made it through successfully and couldn't wait for Don to wrap things up so he could go collapse. But afterward, Don went on about how proud he was of Tony and what a great job he had done. He welcomed Tony to the FBI in a speech that seemed to go on for hours. Tony mustered his inner strength to keep from delivering the contents of his stomach at Don's feet. Mercifully, Don finally handed him a packet that contained his flight itinerary and tickets. A bus would be available to take him from the airport to the training facility at Quantico, the Marine Corps base in Virginia where the FBI conducted training for its agents.

Tony waved at Don as he finally drove off, managing to appear elated. In reality, he was numb and turning colors. Tony trudged toward his car, not making it more than a couple of steps before leaning over, putting his hands on his knees, and throwing up.

CHAPTER 19

Quantico

ALYSSA ACCEPTED THE NEWS THAT TONY HAD MADE IT THROUGH the FBI's rigorous selection process. She knew he was already doing exceptionally well for himself, with his handful of businesses and high-level position at Dillard's. She was uncertain about giving up the security Tony's entrepreneurship offered her growing family. But she also knew he had dreams of his own that she wanted to nourish and encourage. Her upbringing had instilled in her a willingness to let her husband be in charge, and Alyssa was determined to play a supportive role in their relationship. She had resigned to the thought of being without her husband for the four and a half months of training on the East Coast he was about to embark upon, and was prepared to somehow get through it as a temporary single parent to little Anthony. But she was far less certain how the family was going to make ends meet with the cut in pay they would have to learn to live with.

Her apprehensions melded into amusement when she watched Tony set up his video camera on a tripod as he made a series of tapes that Anthony could watch in his absence. "Hi, Anthony, this is Daddy, and even though I can't be with you right now, I'm always going to be thinking of you. I had to go away to work, but I'll be home soon, and we can play together again. Listen to Mommy. You're the man of the house now! Daddy loves you, and I'll see you soon…"

* * *

Tony sat, riveted as he stared out the window as his cross-country flight approached the Washington National Airport, southwest of Washington, DC, in Arlington, Virginia, renamed in 1998 as Ronald Reagan Washington National Airport. He marveled at the famous structures he had only seen in photographs that now lay beneath him. They appeared more like toy models than the real monuments he knew they were.

The jetliner descended, and Tony's pulse raced as those hallowed artifacts came into sharper view, becoming larger and larger, reminding him of exactly where he was and what he was doing. He reflected on all that had led to this point in his life: all he had gone through to make it to America and to become a US citizen, how difficult it had been to take care of himself through high school and college, how he'd become a successful businessman, husband, and father. And now the many roads that had led him to this new reality came into sharp focus. He had willingly sought this mission, a mission fraught with challenge and uncertainty—yet one which, in that quiet moment aboard the aircraft, he resolved he would not fail to complete.

The jetliner glided across the Potomac and made a smooth three-point landing. Tony mused that his FBI adventure was off to an auspicious start as a happy murmur filled the cabin from passengers glad to be on the ground safely. He glanced at the side of the taxiway and noticed it was lined with lush greenery reminiscent of the rainforests in Venezuela he had left so long ago. Tony marveled at the verdant elixir Mother

Nature produces when she is provided an abundance of water and fertile ground. *Maybe this place won't be so bad,* he mused to himself, managing a wry grin observed by no one.

Tony located the bus that would carry him into Quantico, along with other FBI personnel and support staff with the same destination. Soon he found himself firmly on the road to the next chapter of his life.

It was a hot spring day. Tony was content to keep his own company, not joining in with other recruits who chatted away. He opened his window and was taken by familiar warmth and humidity. He would later learn that most people termed this type of climate "muggy." But to Tony, it was just right and made him nostalgic for the Venezuela of his youth.

It was a beautiful countryside, he thought, as the bus rumbled along the thirty-seven-mile drive from the airport to the FBI Academy in Quantico. Tony found the lushness of the landscape alluring. A sweet aroma from the new spring growth of aster, wild ginger, mistflower, and a thousand other native plants wafted into the bus and, in no small measure, lessened his apprehension. A hundred thoughts swirled in his mind. He had read everything he could get his hands on about the FBI. He'd seen every movie ever made about the Bureau and knew full well the dangers inherent in his new job. He was well aware that some new FBI recruits fail to graduate from the Academy. Tony was confident the physical training would not be difficult, but what if he encountered difficulties with translating and assimilating technical material in a second language? What if he found he was not accepted as a foreign-born American? What would happen if he washed out? How would he support his family? Government checks would stop, and he would have to scramble to rekindle his old businesses.

He tried to excise such thinking, preferring instead to latch on to positive, hopeful thoughts. *After all,* he reasoned, *they interviewed hundreds and hundreds of worthy candidates and selected just forty-seven people for this class, and I am one of them.*

Holding on to that notion made him feel much better as the bus turned onto the huge Marine Corps base that housed the FBI's training facility. Quantico was a city unto itself, a home for thousands of military personnel, their families, government contractors, and other civilians. He saw an airfield with military aircraft taking off and landing, including nimble jet fighters that pierced the morning sky with a deafening roar, leaving silvery contrails in their wake. He passed shooting ranges where Marines honed their marksmanship skills with the *pop-pop-pop* of rapid rifle fire. The report of exploding mortar rounds and hand grenades mingled with the occasional unmistakable sound of distant heavy artillery shells finding their marks on a range and generating a booming echo he felt deep within his chest. And everywhere he looked, there were platoons of fit and determined Marines running in cadence. His bus stopped at a traffic signal, and Tony watched a squad pass by his window, singing at the top of their lungs as they jogged:

Momma told Johnny not to go downtown.

A Marine Corps recruiter was hanging around.

Suzy told Johnny go serve your nation.

Take a cab down to the MEPS station.

Lo right, a lo righty lay o.

The platoon held their colors high in proud display as a broad-shouldered drill sergeant ran beside them, leading the refrain.

Tony's bus made its way to the sprawling complex of the FBI Training Academy, an expansive campus with buildings that housed classrooms, conference rooms, a vast auditorium, and two seven-story dormitories. The concrete and glass high-rise structures appeared modern and efficient to Tony, reminding him of the newer buildings at his university in Utah.

A sign read, "Welcome to the FBI Academy." Tony grabbed his small suitcase containing what he'd been instructed to bring, made his way to a reception area, and introduced himself to the attendant. His attention was drawn to a film crew set up nearby. When Tony asked what was going on, he was told that a major Hollywood movie was shooting some scenes for a film called *The Silence of the Lambs*, which would star Jodie Foster. It turned out that she was getting instruction and coaching from the same senior agents who would train Tony and his class.

Tony met Mike Anderson, a tall, thin Southerner and fellow classmate who was already checked in and assigned to help Tony find his way around. Easygoing and friendly, Mike told Tony what room he was in and that he needed to go pick up the uniforms he'd be wearing for the next sixteen weeks. He gave Tony some other necessary information and told him there was a dinner scheduled for new agent trainees later that evening after a mandatory orientation class—with an FBI living legend, Ed Mireles, the supervisory special agent in charge of his class.

As Tony entered the main building for the first time, he was struck by a sense of tradition. The building had an energy to it that stirred in him a deep respect for the history of the FBI. He wondered how many other agents had made this journey before him. He noticed instructors and other senior agents dressed in distinctive colored shirts, setting them apart from everyone else. Tony could not help but imagine the cases they had worked on and what stories they had to tell. Many different classes were going on in different phases toward completion. When he saw trainees who he thought were about to graduate, he wondered what they had gone through and how tough it must have been for them. Some appeared as though they could do a thousand push-ups. Others displayed unmistakable confidence that must have come from knowing they were nearly finished with their training.

On the way to his dorm room, Tony passed the FBI Wall of Honor for the first time and stopped in his tracks. He knew he was on sacred ground as he gazed for the first time at the names and faces of the FBI agents killed in action. These included agents who died in gun battles with suspects or during terrorist attacks. Memorialized here as well were the agents and professional staff who also gave their lives in the line of duty, but not necessarily in an adversarial confrontation. Tony set his bag down, paused, and said a silent prayer for the souls of the fallen, also asking God to protect him and to grant him the strength and courage he would need to succeed. He wondered what kind of mark he might be able to leave upon the institution when his days of service were over. He prayed that he would make a solid contribution.

CHAPTER 20

Special Agent Ed Mireles and the Miami Firefight

THE MID-1980S WERE MARKED BY A DRAMATIC RISE IN THE USE OF cocaine in the US. It became the drug of choice for yuppies and the elite, Hollywood types, college students, and even the poor in inner cities. Miami became a focal point for the importation and distribution of the drug, and cocaine wars among the drug cartels and their gangs proliferated. The rise in cocaine use led to a flourishing of criminal activity of all kinds.

It was a clear and crisp morning on April 11, 1986. The FBI's Miami field office's bank robbery squad had been seeking a pair of bank robbers who were a testament to this upsurge in crime, marked by their ever-increasing use of violence in a string of bank and armored car robberies. The agents were on the lookout for a dark-colored 1979 Chevrolet Monte Carlo and two white male suspects they considered armed and dangerous. The subjects of this particular morning's stakeout, as the authorities would learn, turned out to be a vicious duo that had been on a seven-months-long crime spree. Most robbers go about their business without murdering people. But these killers, operating in broad daylight and with impunity, had left behind a trail of bullets, murder, and mayhem. They shot their way in and out of robberies, with no regard or consideration for anyone. They left enough clues for the FBI to discern a pattern, and a plan was launched to catch them in the act.

Supervisory Special Agent Gordon McNeill was the supervisor of the sixteen-agent Miami Bank robbery squad. Analysis of the duo's crimes indicated that they hit banks and armored cars on Fridays along a stretch of South Dixie Highway. Agent McNeill assigned each of the agents to specific sectors of a five-mile stretch of the highway. Rather than wait for another robbery, Agent McNeill was trying to make his own luck. Based upon a hunch that the stolen Monte Carlo was going to be used in the next robbery, all hands were on the lookout for it, as well as for several other vehicles that had recently been reported stolen.

Unbeknownst at the time to the FBI agents, the criminals—Michael Lee Platt and William Russell Matix—both had military training and expertise and were armed with a variety of carbines, revolvers, and shotguns. The two had met in the military at Fort Campbell, Kentucky. Matix was an ex-military policeman in the Army after serving in the US Marine Corps. Platt was a well-trained ex-Army Ranger.

Special Agents Ben Grogan and Jerry Dove spotted the Monte Carlo sometime around 9:00 a.m. on a busy street in a commercial district of town. The agents tailed the car and radioed to the rest of their squad that they had a visual and were in pursuit. As the agents followed the robbers, the agents' cars formed a procession. Directly behind Grogan and Dove were Special Agents John Hanlon and Edmundo Mireles, followed by

Special Agent Richard Manauzzi, and lastly, Special Agent McNeill, and Special Agents Gil Orrantia and Ron Risner.

The suspects became aware they were being followed and, in a classic countersurveillance move, made several right turns. They ended up on a small street in a residential area, maintaining a slow speed rather than attempting a high-speed escape. They were confident that with the armament they had at the ready, they had an excellent chance to outgun the authorities and make their escape.

Agent McNeill came upon the convoy from the opposite direction and witnessed suspect Platt jamming a high-capacity magazine into a rifle—a Ruger Mini-14 .223 caliber semiautomatic. Agent McNeill later noted that the suspect had a look on his face that was all business, the demeanor of someone who had decided he would kill or be killed. The FBI supervisor knew that they had the suspects outnumbered. Several of his agents were also SWAT trained and excellent shots. But he was also aware that his other agents were at least five minutes away. McNeill decided that his team needed to act before the shooters got back onto the main street with heavy traffic, and before the other agents arrived. Too many civilians would be put at risk if he waited. Attempting to notify his team of agents, McNeill radioed what he had seen.

Unfortunately, the transmission did not come through clearly, so the team only heard the first half when he said, "Just looked at them, they're loading up something in the front."

What the team didn't hear was "...seat of the car. It looks as if they are getting ready to go."

As they headed closer to the densely populated area, Agent Grogan, the most experienced agent on the scene, radioed the team. In the background, they could hear Grogan say, "Let's do it."

Dove replied, "Felony car stop."

Grogan repeated again louder and more clearly this time, "Take them. Felony car stop, let's do it!"

Agent Manauzzi, who was now third in the procession, had already placed his weapon in his lap so it would be easily accessible.

Agent Hanlon and Agent Mireles pulled up beside the Monte Carlo. They began a series of maneuvers to ram it, jerking the steering wheel to the right to smash the FBI car sideways into the Monte Carlo. Agent Mireles was so close he could have reached out and touched Matix, who was driving. Grogan then pulled his car in front of the suspect's at an angle to slow it down and block the escape route. Mireles had a clear shot at the driver and tried in vain to pull up his shotgun and aim. Still, the long barrel and the constant door-to-door collisions made the weapon unwieldy. He couldn't effectively point his gun at the target.

Suddenly, suspect Platt, in the passenger's seat, lifted and pointed his rifle right at Mireles's head. Fortunately, at that exact moment, Manauzzi, following directly behind, floored his car and rear-ended the suspects, sending the Monte Carlo spinning off onto a gravel road. Hanlon and Mireles's car also began to spin and slammed into a concrete wall. The force of the impact launched the agents' weapons out of their hands. Mireles smashed headfirst into the windshield. Agent Manauzzi's driver-side door flew open from the impact, causing his weapon to tumble to the ground.

Out of the dust cloud, the suspects attempted to make their way back to the main road. Manauzzi acted fast and rammed the suspects' car, forcing it to slide off the road and into a tree. The Monte Carlo was pinned next to a parked car on its passenger side. Manauzzi and Mireles's car came to rest on the driver's side, making it difficult for Matix to open his door. Agent Hanlon's car wound up on the other side of the street, where both he and Agent Mireles got out and took cover. Special Agents Risner and Orrantia arrived at the scene and assumed positions across the road some thirty yards away.

The suspects began firing. As Agent Manauzzi bolted from his car, he was hit twice and rolled out onto the street. Bullets flew everywhere. Matix fired his Smith & Wesson Model 3000 twelve-gauge pump shotgun. Agent Grogan returned fire nine times with his Smith & Wesson Model 459 semiautomatic pistol. Agent Dove emptied a fifteen-shot clip on his Smith & Wesson model 459, reloaded, and fired off five more shots. Agent McNeill ran to the front of Agent Manauzzi's car, took cover, and fired his short-barreled Smith & Wesson Model 19 until he was out of ammunition.

Agent Mireles cradled his Remington pump-action shotgun. Agent Hanlon grabbed his backup revolver, a small five-shot Smith & Wesson Model 36, from his ankle holster. Mireles, fueled with determination, decided he needed better cover and ran. He was swiftly knocked to the ground, his left forearm shattered by a powerful round from Platt's rifle. He gazed upward at a crystal blue sky and white fluffy clouds and tried in vain to use his hands to stand up, but his left arm would not work. He later reported that sounds had become muffled, and the barrage of gunfire seemed like it was a long way off in the distance. Mireles tried to regain his bearings, reaching his hand to stop the blood squirting out from the side of his temple, where he had also taken a glancing blow from a rifle round. He felt his energy leaving his body and was sure he was going to die. Yet somehow, he got to his feet.

McNeill made his way back to the cover of his car, his right hand hit and bleeding, with Mireles limping after him. McNeill attempted to reload his revolver and grabbed his shotgun, which was in his car's back seat. He glanced toward the suspects and saw a smiling Platt pointing a rifle at his head. The killer pulled his trigger three times. Agent McNeill was hit in his neck by a .223 round from suspect Platt's long gun, knocking him onto his back, temporarily paralyzing him, and taking him out of the fight.

Platt now laid down a salvo of cover fire and bounded out of the car. Agent Dove, some thirty feet away, fired and hit Platt but did not drop him. The suspect returned fire at both Grogan and Dove. Both agents fired and emptied the clips of their handguns, shooting twenty-four rounds between them. They hit Platt twice, who returned fire relentlessly. Unfortunately, they also failed to bring him down.

Suspect Platt ran toward Agents Dove's and Hanlon's position. Hanlon saw him and fired all five rounds from his backup Smith & Wesson revolver, missing with each shot. Platt stood over him as Hanlon tried futilely to reload, Platt's rifle aimed at his head. Inexplicably, Platt lowered his aim and shot Agent Hanlon in the groin. He turned his weapon on Grogan and Dove, shooting Grogan several times in his body and Dove twice in his head. Both men died instantly.

Platt entered Dove and Grogan's vehicle, hell-bent on escaping. Matix exited the Monte Carlo and climbed into the FBI car alongside his partner. But by now, Agent Mireles had recovered from the initial shock of being severely wounded, settled his mind, and focused entirely on the task before him. These men had not only shot him but had just murdered two of his brothers in arms. The initial fear he had experienced turned to a rage that took over. He resigned himself to the fact that he was likely about to die and accepted it. Mireles rose and used the right rear of McNeill's car to steady his shotgun with his one good arm. He let loose a round of double-aught buckshot that caught Platt in his legs.

As the criminal desperately tried to start the car, Mireles maneuvered the shotgun between his legs and pumped another round into the chamber with his good arm. He mustered the strength and will to rack the shotgun's slide. He managed to fire off three more rounds, every single shell he had loaded, but he did not bring the suspect down. Platt grabbed Matix's revolver and got out of the car, seeking to stop the agent who had been shooting at him. Platt fired three .357 Magnum rounds at Mireles, but fortunately, none found their mark.

Platt got back into the FBI car to make his getaway. Tossing the shotgun aside, Mireles took out his service revolver and aimed as he limped toward his supervisor's car and the murderers who had shot his fellow agents. Firing steadily and purposefully, Mireles let loose two high-grain hollow-point bullets into Platt, three more into Matix, and then another and final round into Platt. Both Matix and Platt were finally incapacitated and later died at the scene. Mireles's determination and dedication to duty had been instilled during his time in the Marine Corps and enhanced by his life in the FBI. He had suffered catastrophic wounds but somehow willed himself to end the gun battle.

The Miami firefight was over and proved to be one of the bloodiest in the FBI's history. In five short minutes, 145 rounds were fired. The gun battle became the focus of numerous investigations and articles that reviewed and dissected law enforcement tactics. The firefight also inspired a two-hour television movie, as well as a segment for a reality-based TV series. More importantly, it led to a review of weaponry and opened the door for the FBI to modernize and implement an array of higher-powered service weapons that allowed future agents to keep up with the increased firepower of criminals on the streets.

Agent Mireles would later reflect that during his twenty-five years with the FBI, he had thought often about the possibility of being involved in a shoot-out like the one he'd survived. He had long ago decided that if anything were to happen to someone, he'd prefer it would happen to him rather than to one of his fellow agents or an innocent civilian. That was just the kind of man he was, a patriot with a deep and abiding love of country and compassion for his fellow man. Mireles, a typically kind and jovial man, was forced into action that morning. Through his strength of character, instinct, and training, he discovered something deep within himself that was unbreakable and, in the process, became a living legend within the FBI.

CHAPTER 21

Sixteen Weeks

IT WAS SOMETHING TONY WAS ACCUSTOMED TO. HAVING A LAST name beginning with the letter *A* always put him in the front row of any classroom he'd ever been in where seating was assigned alphabetically. This orientation class was no exception. Tony sat at the head of the room in the front row and directly under the gaze of the Bureau's living legend. Ed Mireles did not look much different from the photos that accompanied the many articles Tony had read on the microfiche at the library where he'd researched the FBI before joining.

Ed was a big man, who at six feet carried his two hundred pounds well. There was a hint of gray at his temples, his hair parted on the side, cut neat and tidy, and his round, smooth face bore a seriousness which made him look older than his thirty-seven years. Staring down the face of death will do that to you. Tony welcomed the good fortune of having Ed Mireles as his training class's staff counselor, the person ultimately in charge of the whole group.

Ed commanded everyone's full attention as he stood before the class. When it appeared he was about to speak, all forty-seven trainees, clad in identical khaki slacks, tan belts, and dark blue Polo shirts with "FBI Academy" in gold embroidery, straightened in their seats and put their pens to paper, ready to write down whatever Ed had to say. Instead of speaking, Ed Mireles stood and looked the group over a long moment, making eye contact with each recruit. And right when everyone began to squirm in their seats, he managed a wry grin and a snicker. It wasn't derisive, nor arrogant, yet it conveyed Ed's certainty that these people had no idea what they were in for!

He eventually broke the silence and introduced himself. He then had each trainee stand in turn and talk a little bit about themselves. He started in the back of the class, so by the time it was Tony's turn, Tony knew he was among some extremely gifted individuals.

They were attorneys, pilots, MBAs, former military officers, computer experts, and others who likewise had distinguished backgrounds. Every recruit was accomplished in some manner.

"You all can look forward to a schedule that will require physical training in the morning, classrooms all day, followed by firearms training in the evening," Ed announced.

He then went over rules and regulations and recapped the kinds of material they would cover in their sixteen weeks. He told them to be prepared for academic subjects like operations, investigative techniques, law, behavioral science, forensics, counterintelligence, and interrogation. He warned them they were about to undergo many firearm training hours, and they had better qualify with high marks on each weapon the FBI uses: handguns, long rifles, machine guns, and shotguns.

"You'll never know when your life or the life of a fellow agent will depend upon your ability to react and to rely on the training you are about to receive. So you will drill and drill and drill until it becomes second nature," he said.

No one doubted that this man knew what he was talking about.

Ed informed them that they would later put their skills to use during case exercises at Hogan's Alley. Here, trained actors portray bad guys and put them in a variety of tricky situations. It was their job to make sound split-second decisions. He advised them of the ninety rule.

"If you are not familiar with the ninety rule, it means you are allowed one eighty-five on one of your tests, and that's it. Everything else must be ninety or better to pass. So don't use your one and only eighty-five too early."

He noted that everyone had passed the physical training test to reach this point. But Ed made it clear there would be continued physical training and that every recruit would be required to pass each test, including a sprint and a distance run.

Ed Mireles motioned to his assistants, and two voluminous manuals were handed out to each recruit. These three-ring binders contained hundreds of printouts that covered the rules and regulations each agent would be expected to know backward and forward. It was then that Tony realized why Ed Mireles was amused earlier. Tony was not the only recruit who wondered to himself as he leafed through the pages how anyone could possibly memorize all the two binders contained.

"This job isn't for everyone," Ed said flatly, at the conclusion of the class. "Some of you might have just graduated from law school and have never fired a weapon. Others might be combat veterans." He paused for dramatic effect and again made direct eye contact with a handful of the recruits. "But the fact is some of you aren't going to make it. Each and every one of you may get washed out. If you don't score high enough on your tests, I'm here to make sure you'll never receive your credentials. You are vying to become a part of the finest law enforcement agency on God's green earth. The FBI is only interested in the best of the best."

Before dismissing class, Ed advised them to sleep with their manuals that night and begin to familiarize themselves with them. He informed them that at 0500 the next morning, they would be in for a real treat. They were to meet Agent Rogers, not the Mr. Rogers from "the neighborhood" but a rock-ribbed former Marine captain who was to be their physical training counselor, and who would train them as though they were boot camp recruits.

"And as a former Marine, I'm here to tell you that although some of you may think you are in good shape, let's just say there is good shape and then there is Marine fit. Those of you who make it through this training regimen are going to appreciate what it is to be a lean mean fighting machine."

Fortunately, Tony was confident he was in really good shape, and there wasn't too much that concerned him there. Unfortunately, such was not the case for some of his other classmates, who realized they were about to be whipped into the best shape of their lives.

That evening, Tony sorted through the massive manuals that would be at his side every spare moment he had in the upcoming weeks. When his alarm clock buzzed, he quickly dressed, tidied up his quarters, and scrambled downstairs to the cafeteria where an assortment of personnel lined up for breakfast. He stood in line alongside other recruits and seasoned agents dressed in suits. He perused the room and was duly impressed by the caliber of the people he stood among. Recruits from other classes had on different colored shirts. Supervisors were clad in distinctive yellow shirts. Tony selected a few scoops of scrambled eggs and some fruit, careful to eat lightly in case the first day of physical training was to be particularly harsh. He wasn't too hungry anyway, already filled with eager anticipation. He finished and double-timed it back to his room to put on his PT uniform: dark shorts, running shoes, and white socks. He threw on the gray T-shirt and took a moment to glance down to the three bold letters on the front, confident he would earn the right to wear them permanently in a few short months.

Tony got to the designated training area ten minutes early only to find most of his classmates had the same idea and were already assembled. At precisely 0500, Agent Rogers appeared, and Tony was amazed that he looked almost as Tony had envisioned him. He was in his late forties, not large nor tall, but his posture was perfect and his body strong and wiry. He wore his graying hair short, tight, and high in the typical Marine tradition. He had a no-nonsense bearing, his eyes revealing he'd been to war. He'd seen it and tasted it and lived it, and he commanded instant respect.

"My name is Agent Rogers," the FBI Academy physical training counselor said assertively.

To which there was an instant refrain from a handful of former Marine officers in Tony's class, "Sir! Yes, sir!"

This evoked a slight, approving smile from Agent Rogers, who did not let the deference shown by his fellow Marines go unnoticed.

Tony would soon learn the FBI had a symbiotic relationship with the Marines. Not only was the Academy located inside the Marine base, but the Bureau had also become a natural transition for many high-quality former Marines. Tony felt an immediate affinity for this man who, Tony would learn, was fair and straightforward. Although he did seem to show some favoritism to other Marines, he was evenhanded with him. Tony sensed Agent Rogers respected him, or at least never made it a point to single him out. This was owing to Tony's willingness to train hard and not draw attention to himself.

"You people aren't kids," Agent Rogers shouted loud enough to be heard in the back row. "So I'm not going to be a drill sergeant. You're all grown up, and you've all done something incredible to arrive here, I'm sure," he said, taking a long moment to study his charges. "I do have some expectations. I expect you to give me your undivided attention, perform on every test presented to you, work hard, and train hard. In return, I will train you to the best of my ability," he said, pausing for dramatic effect. "I'm sure by now you are all aware that on the physical tests—as well as your other tests in this Academy—when you receive a ninety, you're a C student. If you earn a ninety-five, you are a B student. If you achieve a ninety-eight to one hundred, only then are you an A student."

The first day's training was not difficult for Tony. They did calisthenics with push-ups, sit-ups, squats, and lunges, with plenty of jumping jacks. That was followed by a three-mile formation run, which Agent Rogers did with them, calling out the cadence and ensuring everyone kept up. One candidate who was out of shape and overweight had a difficult time keeping up and caught Captain Rogers's eye.

Each new class is tasked with forming their own slogan representing who they are as a team. The following day, Agent Rogers stood in front of the class, having been informed of their chosen motto, "Leaner, Faster, Stronger." "Let there be no mistake. If you graduate from my class, you will emulate your slogan!" he said. "You are in my class, one of two classes for new recruits. Mr. Sakamoto, a fine instructor, runs the other class. At the end of the training, you will be tested. Your numbers will be compared to Mr. Sakamoto's class. I do not like losing to him, and this class *will* outperform his class! I do not give a shit about what Mr. Sakamoto is doing with his class. Under my command, you will do things my way, and you will do them better than Mr. Sakamoto's class. Am I clear?"

"Sir! Yes, sir!" the entire class responded.

"Those of you who make it through the Academy are going to encounter bad guys out there capable of putting five rounds into your heart and then going out for a hamburger. They are your enemy. They will end your life if you are not mentally sharp and physically strong. You will die. My job is to make sure you are mentally sharp and physically strong so that you will live!"

"Sir! Yes, sir!" the class again responded.

Agent Rogers strolled up to the out-of-shape recruit and grabbed his ample gut. "What is this?" he hollered. "I don't know who let you in here or who your daddy knows, but you will lose this, or you will not be graduating with my class. Besides giving a shit whether you get your goddamn heads blown off, my job is the keeper of the flame," he shouted, clearly annoyed. "We are not going to lower our standards because one of you thinks he can sail through on good looks, charm, or by the good fortune of being born into a prominent family. You meet or exceed our standards, or you...are...done!"

He turned to the entire group, "I don't want to see any of you people taking the elevators. You will walk at a brisk pace everywhere you go when you are inside of a building. Outside, you will run!"

Agent Rogers had the class repeat the fitness tests they all had to pass to be accepted and impressed upon them that they must meet specific goals by the end of sixteen weeks. The out-of-shape recruit failed on his tests, and Agent Rogers told him he had two weeks to pass the basic test, or he would be dismissed.

Tony soon found out that Herschel Walker, the football player, was in his class taking part in a program that let celebrities come in and train with the new recruits. Herschel could run short distances like crazy and knocked all the other tests out of the park. His only weakness, if he had one, was that he wasn't stellar on the endurance runs. One of his classmates turned to Tony as the two of them stood hands-on-knees after a particularly grueling three-mile run at a high pace, and together they watched Herschel cross the finish line later than many other recruits.

"So he's human after all," the classmate offered. Tony, not much of a football fan, didn't know who he was.

Still, he and Herschel got acquainted with one another and got along fine as the class progressed.

A few days later, on another long-distance run, the class neared the top of a long, slow-rising trail. The out-of-shape recruit was wearing out, and the distance between him and the pack was growing. Agent Rogers had seen enough, circled back, and jogged next to the guy, giving him a once-over. The recruit's crimson face was covered in sweat, which cascaded into his eyes as he panted and struggled mightily to stay on his feet.

"What's the matter, son. Are you crying?" The recruit shook his head from side to side, his mouth agape like a hooked fish. "You don't like me? You don't like my training class? Do you want to quit? You're not a quitter, are you?" he barked into the young man's ear. "Because quitters get shot and killed!"

On the verge of fainting, the recruit contorted his face, tried to say something, but was unable to get his words out. He almost collapsed.

Agent Rogers shook his head in disgust and waved up an old military pickup truck following the group. He pointed to the fallen trainee, and two assistants pulled the truck over, picked the guy up, and put him in the back of the truck so the Bureau could begin processing him out.

Agent Rogers rejoined his squad, turned, and ran backward. "Anyone else want to get into the truck? Any time you think you can't make it and you need a free ride back to wherever it is you came from, just jump in the truck!"

The class went on to do many different types of challenge drills and exercises to include a shuttle run. Inside a gym, they would run a compact obstacle course that required tight turns and quick sprints. They would also run 5Ks and 10Ks, as well as the "Yellow Brick Road," a grueling course a little over six miles up and down hills, through woods, mud, and water, over walls, and under barbed wire.

The recruits' usual routine—which included physical training in the morning followed by a day of classroom education and a late-afternoon rotation between firearms training or Hogan's Alley drills—became familiar and all-consuming for Tony. There was little downtime, and the packed schedule kept him going from one thing to another. In his downtime, he read and memorized material from the two manuals that were his constant companions.

Tony and his fellow students were issued training weapons, so they became familiar with handling them, carrying them, and loading them. These training firearms were called "red-handled weapons," and only dummy ammunition was used. Tony practiced clearing jams in the long guns when they were fired on the range and learned how to assemble and disassemble every weapon, including a Smith & Wesson .357 Magnum revolver, a Remington shotgun, and the MP-5 Heckler & Koch submachine gun. He became exceedingly skilled at dumping spent brass out of his handgun and using a speed loader to reinsert new cartridges. He even mastered all of these tasks with his eyes closed, often under the intense pressure of his firearms instructors yelling at him mercilessly as they tried to replicate the kind of pressure one experiences in a gunfight. Fortunately, with Tony's background in martial arts and meditation, he was able to tune out the distractions, stay calm, and perform.

As training progressed, the recruits were given more freedom. There was weekend leave, time to go to the library and study hall, and other privileges, but there was always one restriction: everyone had to be on time, especially to the morning physical training class. There was no official bedtime, but Tony and his peers were aware that each day would be a grind, and they had better be as sharp as possible. Often, they would have to stuff their pockets with whatever they could carry out of the cafeteria and eat on the run.

When Tony's class became proficient with their firearms training and coursework, they were ready to go practice in Hogan's Alley—the city that gets robbed more than any other in the United States. Built with the help of Hollywood set designers, Hogan's Alley is a replica of any small town, complete with shops, a bank, a hotel, houses, and everything one would expect to see in a community, including citizens. There was even an homage to a past success, a replica of the Biograph Theater, where John Dillinger, the notorious bank robber, was killed by FBI agents in 1934. Other agencies also used the town for training, so it was a busy place both night and day, with constant robberies and assaults. There were continual drug deals and spies in the midst of cloak-and-dagger espionage and terrorist operations.

Hogan's Alley was inhabited by government employees—actors who, each day, were given roles to play. In this mock city, Tony learned how to deal with bank robberies, assaults, kidnappings, terrorism, and the gamut of situations he might encounter in the field.

Tony would meet with his fellow trainees, and a squad supervisor would give them a particular assignment. They'd be given a recap of a crime that had occurred, a description of a suspect or suspects, and perhaps a lead as to where the suspect might be. It was then their job to get into their vehicles and go make an arrest. For instance, if a suspect were holed up at a hotel, recruits would have to interview the manager, so Tony and his fellow students received realistic training in many of the kinds of things that were sure to come up in their day-to-day jobs as full-blown FBI agents. The instructors, dressed in their yellow shirts, watched their every move. The trainees were not allowed to acknowledge the instructors, talk to them, or God forbid, shoot them, any of which would result in immediate disqualification and the end of the drill.

Tony soon learned that when he entered Hogan's Alley, anything goes. The performers were there to provide realistic drills, with convincing actors doing the kinds of things criminals do. One time, Tony had to arrest a biker at a pool hall. Unfortunately, it was a real biker who had been given an outline of the script but told to do whatever he would do in real life. The actor might be instructed to reach for the agent's gun and try to shoot him with it. Or he might have been told to try to take an agent to the ground. Trainees began to realize they had to be ready for anything. Both actors and trainees were given a perfunctory warning not to get hurt, but there had been instances where bones had been broken and teeth knocked out. Instructors coached that they'd rather have trainees make a mistake in Hogan's Alley than in the real world. The bullets weren't real, but the adrenaline sure was.

The instructors regularly reinforced, even to trainees who were formerly law enforcement officers, that the Bureau had strict rules to follow. Trainees learned when to pull out a firearm when to keep it holstered. Tony and his colleagues learned techniques to gain people's cooperation without resorting to lethal force.

In a fugitive arrest exercise, Tony's team leader began talking too much to a bad guy on the other side of a door. He refused to open it all the way. Rather than kick the door in and gain entry, the leader tried reasoning with the guy. The bad guy slammed the door in his face and fired shots through the door. The dummy ammunition was designed to make a noise and not leave any mark on the target. Still, everyone knew live ammunition would have penetrated the door and hit anyone on the other side of it.

The instructor jumped in and began pointing fingers at the would-be agents. "Okay, you're dead. You're dead. You're dead," he screamed. "Why the hell would you do that? Why didn't you get in there and knock him on his ass? Now everybody's dead because you couldn't make the right decision!"

Instructors routinely rotated leadership within the training teams to find out who could and couldn't make good split-second decisions in the heat of battle. In one case, Tony's team had a suspect who worked at a factory and was armed and dangerous. Tony had to decide whether to go in during the man's shift and take him down, or to wait for the suspect to come out. Tony decided to stake out the exit and wait the suspect out.

When he did, Tony walked up to him from behind, pulled his gun out, pointed it at the man's center mass from the back, and shouted commandingly, "FBI! Don't turn around! Don't move your head! Put your arms behind you!" He put the man in handcuffs and was ready to shoot to kill had the man made the wrong move.

The instructors were happy about Tony's decision. To go in and shoot up a place and see who's left standing might work in other combat situations, but that's not the MO of the FBI. Tony and his classmates were trained to work smartly and avoid civilian casualties at all costs. They understood that they would be working in environments where they had to respect the law, even in cases where those laws might work against the objective. As an example, in the real-life Miami shoot-out, it was reported that eyewitnesses said they were able to tell who the good guys and bad guys were, because at one point in the firefight, a bystander inadvertently walked into the line of fire. All the FBI agents stopped shooting, while the two suspects continued to let rounds fly in the direction of the agents.

Tony and his classmates were drilled to make those decisions to save people's lives. Society is functioning, they were told time and time again, and they are not to disrupt it. Those split-second decisions have to be made when adrenaline is pumping, and fellow agents' lives are also on the line. Tony's whole mindset changed. Things that appeared simple weren't quite so under fire.

Much of the training was geared to diffuse potentially violent situations at all costs while still meeting basic objectives. The goal was to complete a successful mission and keep casualties to a minimum. Recruits were taught not to become a casualty themselves. It was drummed into them that the criminals on the street don't care if you're a computer expert or a combat veteran. They don't know, and they don't care. You are the person who is going to throw them in jail or put them on death row. They'll try to take you out just the same.

The training at Hogan's Alley was so lifelike that Tony often forgot the exercises were only simulations. In Tony's mind, everything became incredibly authentic. At Hogan's Alley, he knew he was going to walk out of whatever situation was presented to him and his classmates, but he got pretty pumped up performing the mock arrests. The beauty of the training was that it was so close to real-life situations that the lessons he and his fellow recruits learned became rooted.

Tony's class also spent a lot of time going over mistakes agents had made that resulted in someone being killed. They drilled on the tricks criminals had pulled off. They learned how a crook could escape from a pair of handcuffs, how agents had failed in proper weapon retention techniques, and the dire consequences that followed. All in all, the training was complicated and intense. Tony grew to understand why the Bureau only accepted high-level college graduates, those with a demonstrated ability to solve complex problems under pressure. Further, there was the requirement to submit proper paperwork after every exercise, which served to remind everyone what had worked and what hadn't.

Well into the sixteen weeks, Tony believed he was doing a good job and began to see the light at the end of the tunnel. He was ready to earn his badge and was doing whatever he thought it took to get along with everyone in his class. He often spoke in Spanish to Gilbert Mireles, who was another one of Tony's staff counselors. He also spoke Spanish from time to time with a classmate whose first language was also Spanish.

One of Tony's classmates had been accused of smuggling his girlfriend into the dorms and was put on probation. Someone had turned him in, and the man was certain it was Tony. This classmate spread the rumor that Tony was a rat. Before long, Tony began to notice some of his fellow trainees distancing themselves from him. However, he tried not to let it affect him. Compared to some of the things he'd seen in his life already, he reasoned this was just another bump in the road and nothing he couldn't handle.

One day after class, as Tony made his way back to his dorm room, a voice shouted, "I smell a rat!"

Glancing back, Tony saw his classmate coming at him. He lunged at Tony and tried to take him down with a wrestling move. Luckily, Tony had anticipated the man's attack in a split second and swiftly stepped to the side and stuck a leg between his attacker's legs. He reached up with his right hand and hooked the guy around the back of his neck. Using the man's power and weight against him, he neatly flipped him onto the floor.

"Don't fuck with me, motherfucker!" Tony yelled as he pointed a finger into the fallen man's face. Then he walked right up to some of his other classmates who stood slack-jawed, their eyes as big as saucers. "Any of you other motherfuckers want to fuck with me? Let's do it right here and be done with it!"

No one took Tony up on his offer.

Tony collected himself and made his way back toward his room.

One of the guys who had just witnessed what happened edged up as he strode and asked, "Man, where did you learn those moves?"

Tony stared through the man and kept walking.

When he got back to his room, he began haphazardly flinging his things into a suitcase, sure that he would be kicked out. There was a knock on the door, and Tony opened it to see Gilbert Mireles standing before him. Gilbert had taken Tony under his wing, and they shared a supportive relationship. Gilbert came in, shut the door, and sat on the other bunk. As he glanced around the room, his eyes rested upon the suitcase and the scattered clothing around it.

He paused for a long moment, then asked, "Where're you going?"

"I'm out of here. If this is what the FBI's all about, I don't want any part of it."

"You're playing into their hands. Don't give in to that shit."

"What am I supposed to do? Let the guy put his hands on me?"

"No. I'm not going to fault you for that. You didn't hurt him too badly."

"Well, so much for this brotherhood thing among FBI agents."

"There are problems in any family," Gilbert offered, then paused a long moment. "You know anything about the Hispanic lawsuit?" he asked.

"I've heard of it. That's about it."

"Well, a lot of Latinos put their asses on the line to make it happen. And a federal judge ruled in our favor. He said Hispanics in the FBI have been discriminated against, and it has to stop. Before this ruling, we were regularly assigned to what became condescendingly known as the 'Taco Circuit.' Those were shit jobs in shit places that nobody else wanted. But that's all changing now, Tony. We need people like you. You quit now, they win. You gotta make it through. You got to show them that you know who you are. You can do it. You're one of the best in your class."

Adrenaline still coursing through his veins, Tony thought hard about what Gilbert had told him. He was amongst an entire squad of skilled high-caliber men and women. He came to the conclusion that Gilbert was right. This was not the time to let one incident with one person get in the way of his ultimate goal. So Tony stuck with it. Fortunately, no one else messed with him from that point on. In fact, a couple of his classmates who had snubbed him became his friends. Eventually, he and the classmate who had confronted him developed an amicable rapport. Tony wondered why it often takes a good fight to bring people together.

Years later, classmates that Tony stayed in touch with still use their best impression of Tony Montana, the lead character in *Scarface* played by Al Pacino, and say, "Who you think your fucking with? I'm Tony Montana," in a friendly nod to the incident that happened so many years ago. Tony can laugh about it now.

Tony completed his training, scoring high in nearly every category. He finished his physical training regimen, never having once been singled out by the ever-watchful Agent Rogers. Tony worked hard to prove to himself and others that whatever he was to attain within the FBI ranks would be earned and not given. He never sought nor received favoritism from his instructors. He had done it on his own and was set to graduate with his class in a few short weeks. Tony eagerly awaited the arrival of Alyssa and Anthony, who were scheduled to fly out for the graduation ceremony and whom he missed terribly.

CHAPTER 22

Transition

A FEW WEEKS BEFORE GRADUATION DAY, ALYSSA CALLED TONY with sad news. Their neighbor and friend, Richard, had passed away. Richard's wife, Ginger, was en route accompanying Richard's body to Arlington, Virginia, where he was to be buried with full military honors. Tony felt an immediate sense of loss and sorrow for a man he did not know long but with whom he had bonded deeply. The military hero had sensed something in Tony's inner being, and the two had met on that common ground. In Tony, Richard saw a young soldier about to embark upon a career of service as he had many years ago, and Richard had greatly encouraged Tony on that path. For Tony, there was a deep admiration and love for the soul of a man who had been so willing to sacrifice and serve. It was a compelling connection between an old soldier and a newly minted one.

Tony hung up the phone, stunned by the unexpected. His immediate thoughts were of the finality the news had brought, the sudden realization that his friend was gone, and so too were the opportunities to ask him questions or seek his advice or inspiration. Still, he was grateful that Richard had come into his life at just the right time to guide and encourage him to make the right decision to serve. He allowed a cascade of feelings to wash over him as he said a prayer for his friend. He would miss him, but he also understood that Richard was on a journey of his own, and he bid his friend Godspeed.

He hadn't experienced thoughts and feelings like these since his grandfather's death. With both men, he lost someone he admired and loved so much, and it stirred in him his innermost feelings and thoughts of mortality and all that goes with it. Tony's thinking had led him to more of the Eastern notion of reincarnation than the commonly accepted Western concept—that a person walks upon the Earth, passes away, and their eternal soul dwells forever in either heaven or hell, depending on how they conducted their life. Tony revisited this question often, always appreciating the complexities that come with reflection upon this great mystery. Long ago, he had rejected the more conventional view, deciding he was most comfortable with the idea that we are all on a continuous journey of spiritual evolution toward an elusive goal. Each travels at their own pace. Individuals who live well and master life can move on to other planes of existence. And while they're here, they can live happy, balanced, and successful lives, creating their own heaven on Earth. Unfortunately, many fail to progress, and many regress, creating their own living hell.

These ideas seemed reasonable to Tony. He would contemplate them often, always returning to the belief that the many things we are to learn on our journey are far too numerous, complex, and challenging to master in only one lifetime.

In Tony's many prayerful meditations and out-of-body experiences, he perceived inner visions that gave him glimpses into what he would think of as other levels of reality. Like when, at the age of nine, Tony fell back from a swing, hit his head, and was knocked out cold. He watched the scene while floating from above. He saw cousins and friends scrambling around a little boy's body, trying to wake him up. When he first looked down at the limp body, it seemed oddly familiar, yet he still couldn't quite recognize who it was. After waiting for what he thought was an appropriate amount of time, he tried to get his cousins, who were in shock, to continue playing.

"Come on, let's go play!" he said.

It wasn't until his uncles came and scooped up the little boy that he caught a real glimpse of the boy's face and realized that it was him. He floated overhead, following their every move.

They took him to his mother's car, and he was rushed to a nearby clinic. He hovered around the clinic, watching from an aerial view. An abiding sensation of peacefulness overcame him, and he experienced thoughts of profound wisdom, way beyond that of a child. He later regained consciousness, still on an examination table, and was overcome with an overwhelming thirst for knowledge, which stayed within him and would profoundly shape his life.

After returning home, he recounted his out-of-body experience to his relatives who had gathered around him. His recollection of great detail stopped all conversations cold while family members gazed at one another in puzzled amazement. *How could Tony know all of this if he was unconscious?* they wondered. When he recounted precisely what they had said, it left no doubt that something paranormal had happened.

Whether these altered states of consciousness Tony had experienced were wholly subjective or whether they were insights into another objective reality, Tony wasn't entirely sure. Of one thing, he was certain—they instilled in him a gut-level belief that reinforced a principle first introduced to him by his father: we are eternal beings on a spiritual journey temporarily inhabiting mortal bodies.

Tony found comfort in his belief that Richard's soul was in transition toward another rung on his spiritual ladder. Tony would miss his friend, but he experienced an inner peace from the acceptance of the natural cycle of life and death. He reminded himself that every living thing comes into existence, then goes out of the physical world. From the smallest microbe to the largest mammal, the cycle is immutable. We humans are no exception.

He did regret that he would not be able to attend Richard's service, a scant thirty-five miles away. It might as well have been three thousand miles, Tony thought. For even in the waning days of training, he didn't have a minute to spare. He vowed to visit Richard's grave as soon as possible and finished his time at the Academy with strong feelings that Richard had become an angel on his shoulder, giving him an extra push to finish strong.

On graduation day, Tony sat in a large auditorium on the FBI campus next to his classmates, with Alyssa and Anthony in the audience. Floyd I. Clark, deputy director of the FBI, gave the commencement address.

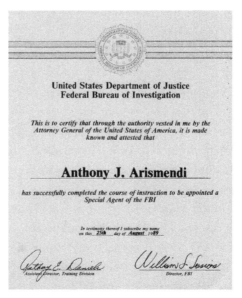

FBI Academy Graduation, 1989

Next on the lectern was the class spokesperson. His speech emphasized the FBI's core values of "Fidelity, Bravery, and Integrity," which is their motto. He then cited the famous quote from Teddy Roosevelt, one that so inspired Tony that he sat upright in his seat as the words resonated in his heart:

> It is not the critic who counts; not the man who points out how the strong man stumbles, or where the doer of deeds could have done them better. The credit belongs to the man who is actually in the arena, whose face is marred by dust and sweat and blood; who strives valiantly; who errs, who comes short again and again, because there is no effort without error and shortcoming; but who does actually strive to do the deeds; who knows great enthusiasms, the great devotions; who spends himself in a worthy cause; who at the best knows, in the end, the triumph of high achievement, and who at the worst, if he fails, at least fails while daring greatly, so that his place shall never be with those cold and timid souls who neither know victory nor defeat.

Tony was so taken aback by those thoughts that he later memorized those lines and recited them often, knowing that the words exemplified the kind of agent Tony wished to become.

At the end of the ceremony, Deputy Director Clark had all the new agents stand and raise their right hands. He then swore them in:

> I, Anthony Arismendi, do solemnly swear that I will support and defend the Constitution of the United States against all enemies, foreign and domestic; that I will bear true faith and allegiance to the same; that I take this obligation freely without any mental reservation or purpose of evasion; and I will well and faithfully discharge the duties of the office on which I am about to enter, so help me God.

Then each new agent's name was called, and Deputy Director Clark shook each hand and presented them a black leather wallet with their badge affixed to an outside flap and their newly earned credentials within. After Tony received his, he returned to his seat and cradled his wallet in both hands a moment before opening it. He took a long moment to study his photograph positioned to the left of the Justice Department symbol. His eyes shifted above the fold to the three-inch-high aquamarine letters stamped over his personal information that unmistakably identified Anthony Arismendi as a special agent of the FBI.

Tony receiving FBI special agent credential from FBI Deputy Director Floyd I. Clark, 1989

Tony allowed himself to savor the moment, now knowing it was real. He had dreamed about this since he was a kid watching American television with his grandmother. Sliding his fingers over the bas-relief of his gold-plated badge, he couldn't suppress a smile. He glanced around and saw the same looks of exhilaration on his classmates' faces, each having fulfilled dreams of their own. He rededicated himself to use his abilities and newly learned skills to become the best agent he could be. He wouldn't disappoint Don, the FBI recruiter, his teachers at the Academy, nor anyone else who had taken a chance on him.

Tony and his dad, Eduardo, at Tony's FBI Academy Graduation, 1989

He glanced at his classmates beside him, many of whom had become good friends, and he knew those friendships would last a lifetime. What great things would they do? What contributions would they make in their careers in service to the Bureau and their country?

Tony would be delighted as the years passed that most, if not all, of these agents would later go on to have a profound impact on the world. Several, including Tony, would make history in some of the biggest organized crime takedowns of our time. Mike Anderson, whom Tony had hit it off with immediately, was handpicked as supervisory special agent to head the Enron task force in what would be the largest and most complex white-collar investigation in FBI history. Another classmate of Tony's went on to snare the notorious criminal Jordan Belfort after a six-year investigation of his dirty business. Belfort's escapades would later be illuminated by director Martin Scorsese in the controversial movie *Wolf of Wall Street*.

FBI Academy Graduation. Special Agent Robert F. Rogers, FBI Academy physical training counselor (center), congratulates newly minted Special Agents Michael Anderson (left) and Anthony Arismendi (Tony, right)

The day after the ceremony, Tony, Alyssa, and Anthony went to Arlington National Cemetery, where they visited Richard's grave. Tony said a prayer, remembering the deep bond he shared with his departed friend. When he finished paying his respects, Tony took his new credentials out, taking another moment to study them, knowing he could not have achieved his goal without the love and support of his friends and family. Tony pressed the soft leather of his ID wallet against the hard granite plaque and said a final goodbye. He wished Richard well on his soul's journey and asked him to remain an angel on his shoulder, looking out for him throughout his FBI career to come.

Baby Anthony and Colonel Richard Beers

Once Tony had settled back in at home, he scooped little Anthony up in his arms and crossed the short landing between his apartment and Richard's. Ginger greeted him at the door as he gave his condolences for Richard's death.

"Come in, come in," she said as she maneuvered her small oxygen tank to the side.

Tony stepped into the small apartment just as he had done so many times before while visiting Richard. Glancing around the room, his eyes focused on the framed photograph of Ginger and Richard on their wedding day.

Searching for the right words, Ginger broke the silence, "Please have a seat, Tony. I have something for you. I'll be right back."

As Tony sat down on the familiar sofa, little Anthony toddled along after Ginger. A few moments later, Ginger came back clutching a stack of what Tony knew were Richard's commendations and medals.

Smiling warmly, Ginger said, "Richard wanted you to have his Bronze Star. You meant so much to him. You were like a son to him."

Awarded in 1970 to Major Richard W. Beers—For heroism in ground combat in Vietnam. Before his death, Colonel Beers told his wife "Ginger" that he wanted Tony to have his Bronze Star Medal with "V" for valor. He received it from Ginger in 1989 after his graduation from the FBI Academy.

Tony was at a complete loss for words. As she extended her arms to him with the medal and citation, he said, "Ginger, you should give this medal to your kids or your grandkids. This belongs in your family."

Ginger continued, "No, he specifically wanted you to have it. You meant so much to him. You were like the son he never had, and he was so proud of you."

Tony was overcome with emotion and fought back the tears that welled in his eyes and silenced his voice. He was speechless and, at the same time, felt honored to have known such an amazing man, a man who had put his life on the line so many times to protect and serve his country. To be given the gift of his medal was more than Tony could take in all at once. Leaning over to hug her, he felt sadness for all that she had been through and lost. He promised himself that although he had been assigned to Arizona and would be moving the following week, he would make it a point to check in on Ginger from time to time and make sure she was all right.

Months had passed, and seemingly out of nowhere, Tony started thinking about Richard and missing his old friend. That night, he had a vivid dream. In it, he was sitting with Richard, who then turned to Tony, reached out to him, and said, "Tell Ginger I love her very much."

The next morning, Tony sat thinking about his dream. He felt the urge to call Ginger to see how she was doing. Tony put it off till the following day when he had more time to visit but then felt an even stronger nudge to call her, almost as if being guided by some unknown force. Deciding to listen to his instinct, he dialed her up. After only a couple of rings, Ginger answered.

"Hi, Ginger, it's Tony."

"Tony, it's wonderful to hear from you! How have you been?"

"Good, everything has been going good over here. I've been thinking about you and Richard lately and what a good man he was. He was a great friend and like a father to me," he said, still unsure if he should share his dream.

Transition | 215

After pausing, he continued, "And actually, Ginger, this is going to sound strange, but I had a dream about Richard, and it just felt so real. Like he was really there. I don't know if you have ever had a dream like that, but I've been thinking about it all morning." As Tony recounted the dream to her, he couldn't help but hear a small gasp from her. He continued, "I woke up this morning and kept getting this nudging feeling like I needed to call you to see how you are doing, but mostly to tell you about my dream."

Caught by surprise, Ginger took a moment to respond but then let out a teary laugh. "Tony, I don't know what to say. Today is actually our wedding anniversary. I've been sitting here trying to get my day started but feeling out of sorts. Some days are harder than others. You know, Tony, Richard never once forgot our anniversary. Not once in all these years. Can you believe it?"

She took a short pause as she thought back on the decades of anniversaries they had shared, and all her many memories of them. She took another deep breath, and her voice lifted a little as she reminisced. "He always found a way to make me feel special and let me know he was thinking of me."

Tony listened intently as she continued.

"Your call today, Tony, is all the proof I need to know that Richard is right here with me and somehow found a way to send me a message on our special day. Thank you, Tony."

Tony couldn't help but feel privileged to have been given the opportunity to deliver a message from beyond for his dear friend.

CHAPTER 23

Breach

THE CROWD OF GAWKERS SWELLED ABOUT THE PERIPHERY OF THE Valley Bank in Scottsdale as though they were preparing to watch the Super Bowl. There weren't enough local police to keep them at bay, and they were in real danger of being hit by stray bullets should a full-blown firefight erupt and move outside. Tony prayed Richard's spirit would be with him this day and blessed his firstborn, asking God to take care of little Anthony should a booby-trapped door explode and hurl him and half his squad thirty feet back into the parking lot, or as breacher if he would take the brunt of an initial ambush. Either way, he was prepared to do his job to the best of his ability and trusted God would watch over him and his fellow agents.

Police and FBI agents stationed in front could see through the thick glass window that one bank robber stood near the main door and held a sawed-off shotgun to the neck of a female hostage. The gun was secured with winds of duct tape that bound the weapon securely to the woman's neck.

FBI SWAT Team. Tony is in the front row, second from the left, with H&K MP-5 and wearing gloves.

Out back with his squad, Tony carefully inserted the key and turned it methodically. This time, he was able to turn the key fully, and the lock clicked open. A wave of relief washed over Tony as he repositioned his MP-5 submachine gun slung from a strap around his neck. As the robber's 5:00 p.m. deadline had just passed, Tony carefully inserted the key into the bottom lock and held his breath while he gently tried to turn it. Nothing moved. He took the key out, slipped it in again, this time wiggling it, hoping he would feel where the key's notches aligned with the tumbler inside.

FBI SWAT Team practicing an explosive entry.

Taking another deep breath, he turned the key again, ever so delicately. He felt some resistance at first, then listened closely for just about the best sound he'd ever heard: a faint *click*. The cylinder miraculously turned, and they were in. He gave the ready signal to Agent #2 behind him, and it was passed down the line. The squad locked legs, interlocking knees in back of knees, until each member was ready to spring into action with Tony's next signal to move.

The unmistakable *pop-pop-pop-pop* of rapid gunfire rang out as all hell seemed to have broken loose from the front of the bank. Tony put one hand on the doorknob and tapped the man behind him on the thigh. He didn't know what was going on out front—his only thought was that they had mere seconds to work their way into the firefight and that lives depended on it. Tony gave the signal to move, and it was passed down the line. When it was returned to him, he opened the door and leaned aside as Agent #2 tossed in a flash-bang grenade. The device deployed an extremely bright light, then a loud bang that temporarily stuns and blinds anyone unprepared inside the building.

In the seconds it took to remove the pin and toss the grenade, the bank robber had opened the front door only a couple inches, stuck his arm out of the small opening, and fired off eleven rounds from a handgun, right before the flash-bang grenade exploded. The grenade exploded with a thundering, concussive *BOOM*! The hostages inside and the crowd of onlookers outside recoiled in shock and dove for cover, reflexively putting their hands over their ears.

Police and FBI agents positioned out front took cover as bullets whizzed by, smashing into asphalt, pavement, and a cinderblock wall. One round found a vehicle parked directly in front of the tire store where the FBI snipers had positioned themselves and shredded its radiator. Amazingly, neither policemen, FBI agents, nor anyone in the crowd was struck by the wild and random shots.

Sam Kincaid and Ethan MacLeod, the two-person FBI sniper team, were at the ready, baking in the afternoon sun atop the Big O Tire store some 150 yards away, with eyes trained on every movement inside the bank. Ethan stared intently through field glasses and gave a second-by-second account of what he was seeing.

Sam was on the scope with his sights trained on the inch-and-a-half gap created between the heavy glass main doors of the bank's entrance.

"The door is opening," Ethan reported calmly.

Sam, taking his turn as the spotter, saw the first bank robber's hand firing the pistol but couldn't see any more of the man through the glass, so he did a mental calculation. He measured up from where the hand was and calculated where the gunmen's head should be. As the gunmen fired his final round, Sam let go a one-in-a-million miracle shot that passed cleanly through the four-inch aperture created by the gunmen's arm and struck him squarely on the tip of his nose. The exit wound through the back of the man's head from the high-velocity round splattered bone and tissue into the face of the female hostage. She was severely lacerated by the impact of fragments of the gunman's facial and cranial bone. None of this was known to Tony or his team entering the back door.

Onlookers in the front of the bank watched the action through the plate glass door in shock as the bank robber's limp body crumpled to the floor in a heap.

The team swept through the near-pitch-black bank with precision as they had relentlessly practiced in hours of intense training, developing fire discipline skills that allowed them to instantly read body language and differentiate robbers from hostages in their meticulous effort to identify a valid threat and avoid shooting the wrong person.

As the team advanced, Tony was responsible for the center field of vision directly in front of him. Uncertain as to the number of robbers and how they were dressed, he was acutely aware that in the dark, they could be easily mistaken for a fellow team member. The place appeared to have been thoroughly ransacked; dollar bills were strewn everywhere beneath their feet as they pressed on. Tony's intuition told him that the robbers were not about to surrender. They were making a last stand and would kill or be killed.

When Tony and his team made their way to the bank's foyer, Tony's eyes focused on the area near the front door. A crumpled body lay on the floor.

A female hostage with a sawed-off shotgun taped to her neck was clearly in shock. She stood holding a piece of the dead man's brain in her hand and yelled, "He's dead. He's dead!"

Knowing now that the gunman had been dispatched, Tony and his team continued to scan the area to identify all persons and determine if they were friend or foe. He noticed a figure dressed in camouflage carrying a machine gun to his left near the front. Two more similarly clad men appeared to be coming from the front of the bank. The presence of individuals armed and dressed in camouflage caused Tony and his team to raise their weapons and prepare to eliminate the threat. But those many days and extensive hours of SWAT training taught them to assess a scene differently. The team had not been briefed or notified that another team of special operators would be entering the bank through the front entrance. However, the manner in which the armed individuals moved and how they held their weapons signaled that they might possibly be a police entry team. Then again, were these highly trained bad guys?

Tony and his team gave commands to the camouflaged men to drop their weapons while panicked hostages cried out. Fortunately, Tony and his team were able to quickly discern that they were on the same side of the law. The men turned out to be members of the Arizona Department of Public Safety SWAT team, who had just arrived and had stormed the front door. The FBI team inside the bank was unaware of this, but training and instincts averted what could have been a tragedy on that brutally hot summer afternoon.

Tony and his men turned their attention to clearing the building as they shouted out, "Stay down! Stay down!"

The Arizona DPS SWAT team brought each hostage out one by one, turning them over to other agents in front of the bank to be brought to safety.

The gunman lay dead on the floor, banknotes and spent bullet casings covering the carpet and polished tile around him like autumn leaves scattered on a lawn. A fine mist of smoke floated like fog, and the faint yet acrid and sour tinge of lead and sulfur wafted through the building.

Once the building was cleared, secured, and the mission had been accomplished, Tony's team stood near one another in the realization that the ordeal was over. At that moment, a spontaneous and cathartic "Yes!" was simultaneously uttered by the men, releasing the tension that had built to an extraordinary level for every squad member.

"Come on, guys. Let's get out of here!" Agent #2 said as he ushered them out the back door.

FBI SWAT—Tony (right), preparing for a hostage rescue operation in a kidnapping and extortion case

The gunfire had stopped, the hostages had been rescued, and word that it was over quickly spread to everyone who had been watching. Onlookers slowly emerged in peekaboo fashion from the cover they had taken. Spellbound with mouths agape, they watched as Tony's team filed out of the building and into the parking lot with their faces and bodies still covered by balaclavas and combat gear.

Amid the chatter from the news reporters, spectators asked themselves in amazement, *Did I just see what I thought I saw? Did that really just happen? I cannot believe they're all walking out alive!* Later, it was confirmed that no hostages or law enforcement were killed in the operation.

As Tony and his team filed around the side of the bank toward the debriefing area, a man yelled out, "Hey, great job, guys!" Drawing the curiosity of the crowd around him, he pointed toward the back side of the bank, where the team was exiting the parking lot. People cheered and clapped. News reporters scrambled to get footage of the FBI team.

The crowd's response evoked mixed emotions in Tony as he made his way to the staging area. He appreciated the respect shown by his fellow citizens, but he also thought, *These people have no idea who I am. I'm your neighbor, the guy down the street with a little kid. I see you in the market.* The crowd was clearly in awe of the agents, but Tony knew that it was indeed God, a whole lot of luck, their training, and most importantly, each agent's willingness to do the deed that saved the day. He knew in his core that he and his fellow agents were fortunate to be alive.

As the team arrived at their staging area, Brennan told everyone to just go to their vehicles, take off their kits, and they would meet and debrief informally at a local spot. Brennan wisely wanted to move his men out of the limelight and into the cool confines of a dark corner of a country-and-western bar that would afford the men the opportunity they needed to talk about what just happened in the anonymity of familiar surroundings. Brennan was leaving it to the FBI bosses and the local authorities to sort out the evidence, write their reports, and deal with the hungry reporters who were grasping every small piece of information they could garner.

As Tony walked to his car, he let out a deep breath and concentrated on bringing his pulse down. Once at his car, he gazed up into a white-hot desert sky, removed his helmet, and placed it under his arm. With his free hand, he gripped the bottom of his balaclava, drenched in sweat, and pulled it up and off of his head. He lifted his face to the early evening sun beginning to fall in the western sky. He thanked God that he could once again welcome the warmth that radiated off his face as he embraced a searing breeze that penetrated his layers of gear and affirmed he was indeed still among the living.

CHAPTER 24

Debrief

IT WAS A DARK, OUT-OF-THE-WAY GLENDALE bar that you would miss driving by unless you knew the place. It was cool and comfortable and, on an evening like this, the perfect private refuge where Tony's team could meet and go over the events of the afternoon.

After each man stopped to call loved ones, Tony's team assembled in the parking lot. They strolled in as a unit. Country music played softly on a jukebox, and the evening news played quietly on the small TV the bartender had mounted on a shelf. The sudden change of air temperature was like walking into a dimly lit meat locker, and it provided a calming coolness that Tony embraced. Day turned to night in an instant, and it took a minute for his pupils to adjust. But he was at ease here. He was among his brothers, out of that ridiculous heat, and in a place where he was free to talk about what they had just experienced. His pulse was back to normal, but the remnants of his adrenaline rush still pumped through his veins.

Word had spread of the FBI SWAT team's successful mission and had just been broadcast over the news as Tony and his compatriots strode in. A few of the patrons had just witnessed the rescue on the bar's television, and unbeknownst to them, these were the same men they had just watched on the screen.

FBI Director William S. Sessions, congratulatory meeting with FBI SWAT Team, Squad Supervisor, and hostage negotiators, sometime after the Scottsdale bank robbery—Tony is in the back row fourth from the left.

The owner of the bar made eye contact with Brennan, nodding in the direction of a back room that he had prepared for their arrival. The men took their seats around a large table, and a waitress appeared with a tray of frosted mugs, then returned with several pitchers of beer and one of lemonade. Tony wasn't really a beer drinker. Actually, he wasn't much of a drinker at all and, at another debriefing on a previous occasion, had ordered Zinfandel. It was the only wine he knew by name and was what

Meeting with FBI Director William S. Sessions, sometime after the Scottsdale bank robbery.

Alyssa drank at dinner parties. On that occasion, the men could not stop laughing about Tony's beverage of choice, and he quickly became the brunt of an onslaught of merciless jokes and good-natured hazing that ended when someone reminded him that "Friends don't let friends drink Zinfandel!" Tony took their ribbing in the spirit it was intended but vowed never again to order Zinfandel, even though he thought its sweet, refreshing taste wasn't so bad.

Tony extended his mug of fresh lemonade toward to the center of the table. Others joined in and clinked glasses. Together, and without prompting, they uttered, "God, luck, and training!" in voices just loud enough for themselves to hear.

Tony lifted his mug to his lips and took a long drink with the others. Maybe it was due to the blistering heat or the high intensity from the

SWAT operation that made him chug the contents of his mug, then go back for a refill. All while his team sat slowly sipping their beers.

The men sat back down in their chairs and drank their beers in a silence that went on for a long time.

It wasn't until the second round of beers arrived that Brennan broke the ice, rising out of his chair. "I am so proud of you guys," he said. "You guys are amazing! Do you realize what we did today? Our first-string team was unavailable, and you guys filled in. Most of you had never been on a mission like this before, and you all handled yourselves admirably. In the finest tradition of this agency!"

Brennan glanced around the table, making eye contact with each man. He bent down and patted Tony on the back like a proud papa. "We are the FBI!" he said. "We are what people think we are!" Brennan's eyes began to mist. "Those people you rescued, they will never meet you. They will never know your names. But we saved their lives out there today, gentlemen. You can be sure of that!"

Tony returned the love, admiration, and respect he sensed coming from his superior. He had been one of the first FBI Hostage Rescue Team members. There were only one hundred in that initial team, one that was ridiculously difficult to get on and became one of the most elite teams in the world. They had trained daily for years all over the world, and the Bureau pulled its future leaders from that team and assigned them to field offices such as Tony's to disseminate their knowledge as team leaders. To receive high praise coming from him meant a lot.

God, I want to be like him, Tony thought. *If I can become half the leader this man is, I'll consider myself a success.*

Brennan stopped a moment and directed his gaze at Sam, the newbie sniper whose miraculous shot had saved the day and undoubtedly saved many lives. "Now, here's a man who defied the odds. How did he do that? He manifested the intestinal fortitude to sit on that scope with his partner in 130-degree heat, and he kept his attention riveted on the possible target. He did not waver. He did not let any thoughts enter his mind other than to complete the mission at all costs. That's what we do, gentlemen. That's what it takes to survive and to be successful."

Brennan paused and again looked his group over for a long while. "And when he saw his opening, he let his training take over. In a heartbeat, he calculated his distance, wind factor, trajectory, and all the rest, and he put that round in the only place that it would be effective. Not bad work for an accountant on his first day as a sniper!"

With that, Brennan raised his glass. "To Sam!"

"To Sam!" everyone echoed in unison, honoring a man who would later earn his way onto the select Hostage Rescue Team in a distinguished career with the Bureau.

The men spent their time mostly talking about their families after Brennan led them through a quick recap of their performance. There were but a few things pointed out that they could improve upon, but generally, he was very pleased with how they executed their operation.

Tony felt a strong bond with most of the men. Like him, most had small children, and the group drifted into chitchat, reflecting on all they had experienced that afternoon. They all admitted that they had said goodbye to loved ones in their minds and come to terms with the real possibility that they might not be returning home. Now that they would once again be able to hug their wives and kids, they acknowledged their vulnerabilities and their gratefulness that they lived to fight another day.

CHAPTER 25

Home

TONY NAVIGATED SURFACE STREETS, TRAVERSING THE URBAN sprawl that was Phoenix. The city had grown to over a million people, and Tony wondered why everyone seemed to be on the road at the same time. After nearly fifty minutes of stop-and-go traffic, he finally made a final turn into Ahwatukee Foothills Village and to the familiarity and comfort that the rows of new white stucco houses provided him. He and Alyssa were pleased to be living in a safe neighborhood in an affordable home, one Tony managed to pay for on his modest salary. The development was tucked up against the taupe-hued peaks of South Mountain Park, which provided a natural protective perimeter that Tony always enjoyed taking in as he drove home. The ever-changing nuances of rock against the sky and the dance of light and shadow took on a vibrant iridescence as a silky sea of white mist rolled up against the mountain, leaving the familiar ridge awash in an otherworldly ocean of clouds.

He waved to a neighbor as he turned into his driveway. For all his neighbors knew, Tony could be a copy machine salesman or an elementary school teacher. They had no idea that he was far from an ordinary guy coming home from work, and Tony wanted to keep it that way.

He stopped in his driveway and looked up to the mountain tops as though for the first time. His vision was sharp, his senses keen—the familiar edge of an out-of-body experience he'd had more than a few times in his life. He felt he was in this world but, for that moment, not of this world.

He walked through the threshold of the front door and paused for a moment. Ninja greeted him first.

Then Anthony, who had heard him come in, yelled out, "Daddy!"

Alyssa rushed up and embraced him as if she'd been sure he would return. Anthony rushed up and threw his tiny arms around Tony's leg. Tony picked his son up and kissed him on his forehead.

"How was your day, little man?" Tony asked.

"I saw you on TV!"

"You did?"

"Yes! Did you get the bad guys?"

"We sure did."

Little Anthony held a piece of paper in his hand. "I drew a plan for you in case you needed it!"

"How thoughtful of you. I'll hang on to it for next time."

Tony carried Anthony back to his bedroom and tucked his son in, drawing the blankets about him like a warm hug. He kissed him again on his cheek. In a soft voice, Alyssa said, "Okay, Anthony, now it's time for you to get some sleep."

Tony kissed his wife and quietly left the room, whispering "Goodnight, little man. I love you."

Tony and his sons at the General Juan Bautista Arismendi memorial. Caracas, Venezuela mid 90s

Tony and his sons during a visit to Caracas, Venezuela in the mid 90s.

He made his way to the kitchen and poured himself a glass of lemonade. He grabbed the book he had been reading, *Autobiography of a Yogi* by Paramahansa Yogananda, and went to his patio.

A short while later, Alyssa opened the sliding door, letting Ninja out on the patio. She then took a seat next to Tony and said, "I was really scared and worried about you today. I was praying that you would be protected and come home safe."

Tony took a deep breath and, as he slowly exhaled, said, "It was an incredibly intense day. I thought a lot about you and Anthony." After a brief pause, he asked, "How are you doing?"

Trying her best to keep from crying, Alyssa said, "I'm okay now. I was so relieved when I saw you come through the door." She grabbed his hand and placed it on her belly so that he could feel the baby. "You feel that?"

"Yeah, I do."

"The baby has been kicking a lot. I think he is ready to come out."

They both smiled. For a while, they sat silently, gazing at a clear and beautiful night sky.

Breaking the reverie, Alyssa said, "I think I'm gonna go lay down. I'm pretty tired. Don't stay up too late, honey."

"Okay, I won't," Tony replied.

Tony scooted his chair out to give himself a better view of the mountains. He began to think of all he'd done, and would ever do, for his beautiful wife, son, and baby on the way. He was certain that God had smiled upon him. Tony vowed to double his efforts to provide for his family, become the best that he could be, and continue on his spiritual journey started all those years ago.

He glanced skyward toward the first sparkling of light in the eastern sky. He enjoyed sitting there at night, marveling at the spectacle of white light cascading from distant stars. Most of the pinpoints of white light he could see were within the confines of our own Milky Way. *This is only our galaxy*, he often thought. *And astronomers believe there are between two hundred billion to two trillion other galaxies out there. Most are bigger than ours.* He would laugh to himself as he considered that most people think Earth is the center of it all!

He lingered there for a while, accepting that such mysteries can never be fully understood with the rational mind. He again thanked God for the gift of life and hoped, as philosophers have supposed, that while we're here, we remember to forget or forget to remember what lies beyond. And maybe at some point in our spiritual journeys, more will be revealed to us.

His eyes caught sight of a rabbit darting from the protection of a manzanita plant and scampering off into the darkness. Living in the desert had made Tony acutely aware of the different kinds of wildlife with which he shared the hot and inhospitable Arizona environment. They were creatures that adapted over the millennia to survive and flourish—perhaps not unlike Tony himself, who had learned to survive and prosper. Tony thought of himself as a guest in their world as he had been a guest in a new country. The screeching of a hawk on the hunt, the call of a quail on the ground, or the howl of a coyote in the distance were the familiar sounds that reminded Tony he was home. This evening was no different than others he had spent here, except that his senses were heightened, and he could feel the energy of the lifeforms around him with a renewed sensitivity and a deep feeling of connection and oneness with it all.

He reviewed the trajectory of his life and what had brought him to this place, so distant and different than his birthplace. He thought of his grandmother and her cozy little room furnished with the items that made her happy and the joy he would feel sitting next to her there. He remembered the scent of the room, a combination of cologne and a musty redolence of the ancient caftan she wore. He silently thanked her for the many times she smuggled him into her space to watch the tiny TV that inspired him to become an American and an FBI agent.

Tony thought about the hard times he went through and some of the people he encountered, some who treated him well and others who did not. He understood in his core that all humans, even the worst of them, also have good inside. He wasn't bitter about having personally experienced discrimination. He believed people were, for the most part, just acting out their insecurities or reverting to their tribal nature, where survival demanded instantly ascertaining whether someone is friend or foe by the look of them. He had resolved a long time ago not to let any of that hold him back. There would be no excuses, he had decided. He would simply outwork and outhustle and outsmart anyone who thought less of him because of his cultural heritage, ancestry, or accent. He would never hold a pity party for himself—he would lead by example and succeed in spite of any obstacles put in his way.

Tony reflected on his journey with the Bureau thus far and was proud that he had completed his training and was well underway on his career path. He had completed all the requirements of the *New Agents Training Manual*, and his supervisors had signed off, giving him good marks and, in some cases, high praise.

But with his business and accounting background, he had spent too much time, he thought, on the white-collar crimes squad, where he feared being stuck. He had spent a few months in the Phoenix field office pouring over balance sheets and accounting books and had grown weary of the thought of becoming a bean counter—not part of the real action. At one point, he contemplated leaving the Bureau and joining the DEA to escape the monotony of meeting after meeting in which lawyers and accountants discussed the intricacies of paper trails and money laundering. He would often have to pinch himself so he wouldn't fall asleep during meetings that droned on and on. Not that he didn't respect the people he worked with. In fact, he held the people who made up that squad in high regard. In his mind, they were accounting and business Jedis, most with advanced degrees and years of experience. And intuitively, he knew that following the money was crucial in bringing criminals to justice. Tony was confident, however, that he possessed a certain kind of skillset that would be better utilized in the field. A deep-seated yearning was calling him to go undercover.

In his new agent training, Tony was exposed to different facets of the profession. He thought that the Bureau's requirement for each new agent to get a taste of every department was an excellent idea. He worked on the white-collar crimes unit, the bank robbery squad, the SWAT team, and did counter-surveillance and undercover work. Like other new agents, he was always anxious to get his feet wet and would volunteer for any assignment where more seasoned agents let him do something that he hadn't done before.

DEA Special Act or Service Award

Medal of Meritorious Service

The first time he did undercover surveillance was in an ongoing investigation of Charles Keating, who had been implicated in the savings and loan scandal that led to Keating's eventual conviction and imprisonment. He didn't mind sitting hour upon hour in a cold car, sipping coffee, and holding binoculars to his eyes as he surveilled Keating's home from afar. It was much preferable to sitting in those interminable meetings. Experiencing the kinds of things other undercover agents did ignited a fire in him.

Tony was confident that his background on the streets of Venezuela gave him special value to the FBI. His command of Spanish was such that he was able to alter a dialect ever so slightly to sound like a native of practically any Spanish-speaking city in the world. He knew he had skills that could be best put to use in the field. Undercover work and undercover operations was where he belonged—he believed—and where he would end up if he had anything to say about it.

Receiving the Hispanic Police Officer Command Association Medal of Meritorious Service from DEA Special Agent in Charge Errol Chavez.

That is what happened. During his two decades in the FBI, Tony had many opportunities to put his talents to work as an undercover agent. He experienced many situations where the slightest mistake would have resulted in instant death for him or for his fellow agents. He developed alter egos and learned how to turn on different characters within himself so that he could effectively con the cons and bring them to justice.

Tony usually portrayed a midlevel soldier. He learned never to play the head guy, which always afforded him an out, so he never had to make critical decisions on the spot. When asked by the targets of the investigation to take any action that would be considered illegal, out of policy, or could negatively impact the case being built, Tony would respond that he had to check with his bosses. The targets were usually midlevel managers themselves with a chain of command and would understand the absolute necessity to seek approval from bosses before taking action. This would allow time to determine how to best respond and gave him an out. He became an actor, playing roles where there was no second take or a director to yell cut. He had to do it right the first time or face deadly consequences.

As he began to rack up some significant cases, his FBI superiors took notice and began delegating him more authority. With their support and trust, he was able to get his usually large budgets approved and all the time he needed to create and set up an operation to infiltrate a crime organization. Without his superiors' confidence in him, he could not have pulled off some of the elaborate operations that he did. In the process, he was able to supervise and train scores of other agents.

Tony liked to work outside of the box and became an expert in casting elaborate stings at a time when the FBI was refining the protocols for undercover agents that are in place today. He became an expert at using any tool at his disposal to figure out the mindset of a target. Much like a film producer, he would have to write a script, prepare a budget, and most importantly, recruit fellow undercover agents from anywhere and everywhere within the Bureau to play a particular part in his movie. He did it year after year in case after case and managed to put a large number of criminals away, usually leaving his supervisors asking themselves, "How in the hell did he pull that off?"

Tony applied his lessons from producing and managing numerous undercover operations to assisting in writing a manual for the FBI on the best practices for managing informants and overseeing undercover operations. To the agents he had the privilege to lead, he did his best to pass on lessons he had learned from the SWAT team. He worked to instill a desire in his teams to be the very best agents and people they could be.

He encouraged them to cooperate with other divisions of the FBI and federal and state law enforcement organizations with the ultimate goal of serving the American people by removing criminals from society. In his years of service, he did his part to help keep the fabric of society intact along with the dedicated people of the FBI, the doers of deeds who chose to enter the arena.

Epilogue

It was a combination of things that motivated me to become an FBI Agent. The goal of serving was already wired in me. The stories about my family history—knowing that Juan Bautista Arismendi and his wife Luisa were two key and prominent figures in the South American revolution as the general in command of the armies under Simón Bolívar (the George Washington of South America) and as the beautiful heroine with an indomitable spirit who defied the Spanish Crown and inspired a new continent of nations—always filled me with a sense of pride, duty, and destiny.

I loved my career. I loved what I did. I loved that I was able to contribute in a unique way. I understood the nuances, things that can be the difference between success and failure, and I saw things that other people didn't. A lot of it was due to growing up in Venezuela and having to learn the way of the streets. Many of my superiors recognized that, so I had a lot of latitude and was able to create my own reality within the FBI.

During my career, I went after large-scale organized crime, drug cartels, gangs, violent criminals, and terrorist organizations. I was an outsider with a different perspective, working undercover, creating, producing, and directing undercover operations.

I developed an understanding that required the kind of creative process that a movie director, musician, or even an artist uses. I learned how to employ strategies that were outside of the box.

I could look at a situation from different angles and then find a creative way to get in.

I never took no for an answer. Once I had devised a plan to go after a criminal or an organization, I would construct a viable argument with a realistic budget, and I would present it to my superiors for their blessing. As my experience within the Bureau grew, this process became easier, as I was able to prove my methods worked. I was always putting myself in the mindset of the criminal. I had to learn how to think like a criminal. *Who are they? What motivates them? How can I influence them?* I had to get them to laugh, to cry, and to go along with me.

I got a tremendous amount of satisfaction in serving and helping the country that took me in. I honestly feel I made a difference, and I was able to have an impact. I put people in prison who, without me, never would have ended up there. These were individuals who were serving no other purpose than hurting others for their own gain.

I mainly went after crooks who had been on the radar a long time but who no one could ever really get. To do so, I was forced to get creative. It was challenging. It was fun. It was interesting. It was intellectually stimulating in so many different ways. And it was dangerous.

Tony meeting with FBI Director, Louis J. Freeh, during an FBI undercover operation

Tony briefing his supervisor during an FBI undercover operation

Money seized during one of Tony's undercover operations

With taskforce agents, during an undercover operation.

With FBI and Task Force agents, during an undercover operation.

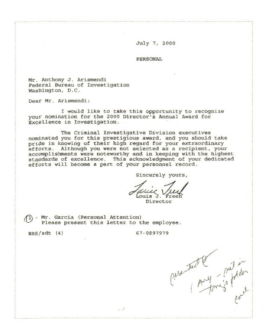

Tony was recognized by FBI Director Louis J. Freeh, for his nomination to the prestigious FBI Director's Award for Excellence in Investigations.

Epilogue | 249

I loved it, and I had a knack for it. I could think on my feet very quickly, and I could see various scenarios playing out in my head. I was able to examine what was happening from the perspective of every person involved. If we pay attention more to our surroundings and to what other people are feeling, we're going to learn a lot. In my business, it was vital to get a feeling for your adversary. You walk into a room, and you have to take in everything at once. Every element of a situation tells you something about the person you're going after.

And so I made it my quest to try to understand everyone I interacted with, especially the bad guys. *What makes these people tick? Why do they do this? What aspect of their psyche is it feeding?* I would try to peel the layers off so I could really get to know the person I was trying to take down. I became an amateur psychologist, sociologist, and even an astrologer. I wasn't trying to diagnose them or use medical terms. I just wanted to understand their motivations fully. What got this person there? Where did I think they were going? And then I would try to predict their next move. Once I figured that out, I would assess how I would counter that move. I was always playing a chess game. It was fun, it was stimulating, it was stressful, and it was scary!

And yes, it took its toll on my family and our personal lives. We paid a high price—having to constantly move, the trauma of overexcitement, constant danger, the stress and uncertainty—living on the highs and lows of life. Toward the end of my career, Alyssa and I parted ways, becoming part of that substantial percentage of marriages involving law enforcement and military that don't last. Through it all, the ups and downs, we managed to raise our two sons—kind, intelligent, beautiful, and amazing human beings.

My brother and I reconciled with our mom within a year after we first arrived in the United States. We had kept in contact with her and my sisters through letters and occasional phone calls. A few years later, and just before I graduated from college, my mom and sisters made their first trip from Venezuela. As the political and economic situation continued to deteriorate and Venezuela began to collapse, my mom and sisters fled to the US. And we banded together to help them—my dad, my brother, and me.

Would I do it all again? In a heartbeat! I came to the greatest country in the world with nothing, not speaking a word of English, became a US citizen, and went to work for the premier law enforcement agency in the world. It just doesn't get any better than that! An extraordinary adventure indeed my life has been. To have been an FBI agent was beyond my wildest expectations. I went for it, and it happened. And I feel very fortunate and honored that I was able to serve and give back to the country that embraced me and has given me every opportunity.

Through my years with the FBI and everything else, I learned a lot about myself and who I really am—an eternal spirit having a human experience. The danger, stressful situations, and adversity actually brought out the spiritual side of me. Luckily for me, it opened me up and made me into a better person, for which I'm grateful.

—Anthony J. Arismendi

APPENDIX I

Juan Bautista Arismendi

JUAN BAUTISTA ARISMENDI WAS BORN IN 1775 ON ISLA MARGARITA, a 390-square-mile island off Venezuela's northeastern coast, nicknamed "The Pearl of the Caribbean" by Christopher Columbus after he landed there in 1498 and found the waters surrounding the island rich with pearls. Arismendi was from a wealthy and powerful family and a *criollo*, a member of the second-highest-ranking caste in the Spanish social hierarchy in the New World. At the top of the ladder were the *peninsulares* (colonists born in Spain). Next in line were the criollos, who were the descendants of the peninsulares born in the colonies, followed by Amerindians, Africans, and those of interracial heritage.

The Arismendi family had been in the New World since the 1500s and was fiercely loyal to the Spanish Crown. Years later, when Tony was on an FBI assignment in Spain, Spanish officials showed him documents over four hundred years old that confirmed one of General Arismendi's forebearers had been assigned by the King of Spain to work as a government official in the colonies.

Eventually, the same issues that spawned the American Revolution came into play for America's southern neighbors. These issues included severe trade restrictions that benefited the mother country, as well as high taxes imposed on the residents of the colonies.

It was a shift in power on the European continent that set the stage for Spain's American colonies eventually breaking from the mother country. Napoleon Bonaparte ascended to the position of First Consul of France in 1799 and immediately took steps to stabilize France's finances, overhaul its bureaucracy, and form a well-trained army. War broke out in 1805, which saw Napoleon soundly defeat the combined Austrian and Russian armies at Austerlitz. Later that year, the combined French and Spanish fleets were defeated by the British Royal Navy, which established mastery of the seas and prevented a French invasion of the United Kingdom.

Soon thereafter, the British established a blockade of French ports. As a response to the blockades and as part of a plan to defeat Britain by destroying its ability to trade, Napoleon established orders that forbade any European country, whether a French ally or a neutral country, from trading with Britain. The orders required any commercial vessels wishing to do business in Europe to first stop at a French port. This system of trade control became known as the Continental System. The two biggest violators of this new trade system were Portugal and Russia. Portugal openly refused to join the Continental System, being a close ally with Britain.

Following French victory at the Battle of Friedland against Prussian and Russian forces, Napoleon and Emperor Alexander I of Russia signed the first Treaty of Tilsit. This treaty ended the war between Imperial Russia and the French Empire and established a new alliance between the two empires. It also rendered the rest of continental Europe almost powerless. France pledged to aid Russia against the Ottoman Empire, while Russia agreed to join the Continental System of trade against Britain. This new alliance freed up French troops, and Napoleon moved those extra troops into Spain to prepare for an invasion of Portugal.

In July 1807, Napoleon ordered Portugal to declare war on Britain, close its ports to British ships, and detain British subjects and sequester their goods. To enforce this order, a sizable French force under the command of General Jean-Andoche Junot occupied Lisbon on November 30. A war between France and Spain on one side and Portugal, England, and Ireland on the other broke out in 1807 for control of the Iberian Peninsula. The war came to be known as the Peninsular War. But Spain soon proved too much of an unreliable ally for Napoleon Bonaparte, and as a result, in early 1808, Napoleon ordered French armies to invade Spain. The Grandee Armee soon controlled most of Spain, including Madrid. A Spanish government was established in exile in Cádiz but was penned in by a major French force.

Meanwhile, the British and Portuguese, who had been pushed out of the peninsula, reestablished effective control over Portugal. This allowed a base of operation for allied forces to move against the French within Spain. At the same time, Spanish armies and guerilla forces engaged and tied down significant numbers of French troops.

To better control Spain and to levy troops for his armies, Napoleon recalled both Charles IV, former King of Spain, and his son, Ferdinand VII, to Paris. He then placed his older brother Joseph on the Spanish throne as Jose I. Joseph's control over the country was tenuous at best and required French reinforcements to allow him to stay in power.

On May 2, 1808, citizens of Madrid rebelled against the French occupation. The rioters were brutally crushed by French foot soldiers and trampled by cavalry charges. Those Spanish rioters captured on May 2 were executed by the hundreds the following day. Spanish resistance spread, kicking off what would become known as the Spanish War of Independence.

The Peninsular War served as the trigger for the fighting that would consume Spain's South American colonies. In response to Napoleon's placement of Joseph on the Spanish throne, individual Spanish provinces established their own ruling councils, known as juntas. These juntas eventually united to form a Supreme Central Junta and offered representation to the South American colonies. This central junta supported Spanish efforts to defeat the occupying French forces but was dissolved after the larger Spanish army was soundly defeated at the Battle of Ocaña.

Seeing the dissolution of a central junta as an opportunity, in 1810, both New Granada and Venezuela declared their independence from Spain. Juan Bautista Arismendi served as a colonel in the militia that defended Isla Margarita, the same military force his father had commanded. He supported Venezuela's efforts to be free from a mother country that looked down on the colonists and discriminated against them because of their place of birth.

Despite the struggle for independence from the French occupation of Spain and the Spanish monarchy, the mother country still viewed the people of their American colonies as second-class citizens, even those citizens of Spanish ancestry born in the colonies (the aforementioned criollos). The Cadiz Junta, formed following the dissolution of the Supreme Central Junta, was heavily influenced by the Spanish Cadiz merchants who favored government monopolies controlling colony production and trade. They could only grow crops not grown in Spain and were not allowed to trade with any countries other than Spain. Representation at the Cadiz Junta was also slanted, providing just thirty seats to colonial representatives (out of 280), despite the colonies having seventeen million inhabitants to Spain's ten million. The system continued the exploitation of South American resources and labor, all to the benefit of the mother country. The people most impacted by the exploitive policies toward the South American colonies were the criollos, turning them into the most vociferous proponents of independence.

A national congress for Venezuela was formed in 1811, which voted for independence on July 5, 1811. In 1812, Colonel Arismendi fought in the Guiana campaign in the eastern sector of Venezuela during the period referred to as the First Venezuelan Republic. On March 26, 1812, a massive earthquake struck the Caracas area, which devastated the city, leaving over twenty thousand dead and much of the city in ruins. Royalists explained that the earthquake was divine punishment for the rebellion against the Spanish Crown. This narrative was advanced by the local Catholic archbishop, the dominant religion of the region. Ultimately, support for the First Republic of Venezuela ceased. As a result, Royalist forces gained control over much of the areas they had lost over the preceding year, including Isla Margarita.

With the Royalist forces reestablishing control of the island, Juan Bautista Arismendi found himself jailed for his revolutionary activities. By 1813, however, the tide had turned, and the Royalist forces were expelled from the island. Colonel Arismendi was freed from jail and appointed governor of the island. The Second Republic of Venezuela, declared and established by Simón Bolívar, was short-lived. Isla de Margarita, however, remained under the control of Governor Arismendi.

In March 1814, Spanish forces had pushed the French occupying forces from Spain, and King Ferdinand VII was restored to the Spanish throne. This change was significant since most of the political and legal reforms in Spain and her colonies were made in the name of King Ferdinand VII. The rebellious activities by the Spanish colonies against the Crown occurred while it was occupied by a French usurper and would be forgiven as long as the colonies fell back in line under the authority of the King. With the support of conservative members of the public and the hierarchy of the Spanish Catholic Church, Ferdinand repudiated the Spanish constitution and ordered the arrest of liberal leaders. Former legal codes and political institutions, including strict administrative control of the colonies for the benefit of Spain, were restored. The hope was that the South American colonies would be governed by a representative government rather than by an absolute monarch. In fact, Ferdinand embarked on a program of strict actions designed to bring the rebellious South American colonies to Spain's heel.

To pacify Venezuela and retake New Granada, in early 1815 Spain organized the largest armed force it had ever sent to the New World. Ferdinand VII assembled a massive contingent of veterans of the campaigns against Napoleon and placed them under the command of General Pablo Morillo. A total of 12,254 troops departed Cadiz on February 17, 1815, aboard twenty warships and fifty-nine transports. The seventy-four-gun San Pedro Alcantara served as the Royalists expedition's flagship. Morillo landed at Carupano, on the mainland of Venezuela and across from the Isla de Margarita, and joined forces with General Morales's five thousand troops, with the initial goal of retaking the island from the control of Juan Bautista Arismendi.

Early warning of the arrival of Morillo's force had reached Arismendi. He assembled a war council to discuss the situation. The island had only two thousand troops and dim chances of relief from other patriot forces. Facing overwhelming odds and consulting with his war council, Arismendi made a calculated decision to cooperate with the Spanish with the aim of preserving his troops, his island, the inhabitants, and his station so that he would be in a position to carry on the fight when the time was right. He concluded that the wisest course of action at that point was to try to negotiate an agreement with General Morillo.

In April 1815, Governor Arismendi met with General Morillo and discussed the situation on the island. He was able to negotiate a peaceful transfer of control and the evacuation of certain individuals, including General Bermudez. Arismendi was replaced as governor by a Spaniard who fell under Morillo's command. Still, he managed to convince Morillo that he was loyal to the king and that his past rebellious activities were focused against the usurper Jose I. Because of this, he was allowed to remain free on the island. The 2,000-man militia was also permitted to stay on the island and remain in possession of their weapons. All remained peaceful on the Isla de Margarita until September 1815, when other officers convinced General Morillo that Arismendi was indeed a threat and Morillo ordered his arrest.

In March 1815, Napoleon Bonaparte—who had been exiled to the island of Elba—escaped his confinement and triumphantly returned to France. The French monarch, Louis XVIII, fled Paris. In an attempt to solidify his power in Europe, Napoleon marched his armies to Belgium to face off with coalition forces. On Sunday, June 18, 1815, the French forces were defeated by the British and Prussian armies. In the coming days, Napoleon reluctantly abdicated his position as emperor and fled France with the intention of reaching the United States. He was, however, captured by the British and ultimately imprisoned for the remainder of his life on the island of Saint Helena.

Nations around the world celebrated Napoleon's abdication, and Venezuela was no different. On September 24, 1815, Arismendi and his young wife, Luisa Cáceres de Arismendi, attended one such celebration, as had many of the island's most prominent residents, including the ruling Spanish representatives. As they enjoyed the festivities, Arismendi was pulled aside by a young man, Pedro Berroteran, and warned of a Spanish plot ordered by General Morillo to arrest him that very night. Luisa implored her husband to flee, but he refused, not wishing to leave without her. She assured him that the Spanish would not take her, a very young woman, several months pregnant. Reluctantly, he consented. As Spanish troops surrounded the building, he climbed to the second floor and slipped into a room. Seeing no other way out, he climbed over the balcony and leaped down, landing on the hard cobblestone street, and sprained an ankle. He hobbled off quickly to escape the contingent sent to capture him.

Since having been displaced as governor, he had maintained regular contact with the island's militia, who had remained loyal to him and the cause of independence. He met with a small detachment, including his son from his first marriage, and moved out. The group stormed a command post and took Spanish captives, including the officer in charge. The small band, along with their prisoners and captured weapons, moved up to the Copey Mountains. Arismendi and the island's local militia had been raised and trained on the island. No one knew the island and the mountains better. The vastness of the mountains would allow Arismendi and his men plenty of room to hide and pursue a guerilla war while he recruited forces.

Unknown to him at the time, the Spanish officials imprisoned his wife, Luisa, in an attempt to extort his surrender. She was held on the island in the castle of Santa Rosa for over a year. While she was held captive, General Moxo, a subordinate of General Morillo and the primary driving force for the plan to take Arismendi into custody, pressured Arismendi's wife to tell her husband to surrender.

When he learned that the Spanish had taken his wife captive, Arismendi was absolutely enraged. They promised to execute her if he did not surrender himself. But the brave and beautiful Luisa Cáceres de Arismendi had help sending messages to her husband, imploring him to keep fighting for liberty.

Arismendi built his forces—predominantly members of the militia he had commanded prior to the revolution—to approximately 1,500 well-trained troops. With the command of the patriot troops on the island, he assumed the rank of general.

During the year 1815, the patriots in both New Granada and Venezuela suffered defeats at the hands of General Morillo. The Second Republic of Venezuela had ceased to exist, and the remaining patriot leaders were fighting amongst themselves, Simón Bolívar was in exile, and the independence movement appeared all but finished. But there was still a glimmer of hope—Arismendi and the island of Margarita.

In late November 1815, General Arismendi held the Spanish forces in place while he performed a sweeping flank maneuver that rolled up and destroyed nearly the entirety of a 900-man Royalist force on the island.

On December 20, 1815, General Moxo issued a proclamation to the citizens of the island, which offered clemency for those that would give up the fight and turn themselves in. If they did not, he promised bloodshed with the blame placed squarely upon General Arismendi. The following day, writing from his headquarters in the Copey mountains, General Arismendi prepared a proclamation that was distributed to the island's inhabitants. He was conscious of the plight the civilians were going to suffer at the hands of the Royalist forces, but he assured them that the forces he commanded were going to fight—Morillo had given them no choice.

Morillo understood how pivotal Isla Margarita was to the rebel cause. The early victories by General Arismendi were providing much-needed hope and buoyancy to the sinking rebellion—that sense of hope and confidence it needed to be stopped. He immediately sent additional reinforcements to the Spanish commander on scene. The patriot and Royalist forces clashed several times in late December 1815 and throughout January 1816. Remarkably, the outnumbered troops led by General Arismendi were winning control of the island. By March 1816, the Royalist forces were holed up in several forts on the island.

During this same time, Luisa remained captive in the castle at Santa Rosa. Despite the horrific conditions she faced while in captivity, she had managed to enlist several women who worked within the fort to pass messages outside, including vital military intelligence, to her husband.

Some of her messages were intercepted by the Spanish. In the messages, Luisa repeatedly encouraged her husband to fight for the liberty of Venezuela. General Salvador Moxo was so incensed by the courage she displayed and the contents of the messages that he proposed to execute her.

Despite the attempts by the Spanish to quash the rebellion on the island, the news of the patriot victories spread throughout the Caribbean, reaching Simón Bolívar. Having fled Venezuela and New Granada following the collapse of the Second Republic of Venezuela, Bolívar found himself in exile in Haiti. But word of General Arismendi's victories provided tremendous encouragement to Bolívar. So much so that he planned to land on the island and meet with General Arismendi himself.

Wishing to dampen Arismendi's success, General Morillo threatened that all persons assisting the rebel cause would be punished with death upon his return to the island. Other military engagements occupied Morillo's time, but he kept his promise, returning to Isla Margarita with a formidable army. Morillo's army was defeated by General Arismendi, and he was driven of the island.

Isla Margarita welcomed Simón Bolívar in early May 1816. Top generals and senior officers in the patriot armies were gathered along with the leading civilians on the island. In a momentous meeting, General Arismendi, in an impassioned speech before the attendants, implored all to vote to recognize Bolívar as the supreme chief and leader of the South American revolution.

General Arismendi continued to serve the cause of liberty and continuously demonstrated unwavering loyalty to Bolívar—a rare trait indeed. In 1876, he was buried in the National Pantheon in Caracas and recognized as one of the leading figures of the South American Revolution and a founding father of Venezuela.

APPENDIX II

Luisa Cáceres de Arismendi

TONY'S GREAT-GREAT-GREAT-GRANDMOTHER, LUISA CÁCERES DE Arismendi, became as famous or perhaps even more so than General Arismendi in her own right, later also recognized as a true heroine of the revolution. She was of the criollo class, born in Caracas in 1799. Her father, an educated and affluent man, saw that she was well educated. When she was still a young girl of eight, the French, under Napoleon, invaded and took over Spain. Napoleon's brother, Joseph, usurping the Spanish throne did not sit well with people in the colonies any better than it did among those in Spain. The French occupation of Spain lasted some six years, but by 1812, the patriots of Venezuela took advantage of Spain's weakness to declare their own independence.

Luisa met then Colonel Arismendi at a Christmas party in 1813. The party occurred shortly after the death of Colonel Arismendi's first wife, Maria. He was immediately taken by Luisa's beauty, keen wit, and composure. It took no time for Colonel Arismendi to embark on a courting campaign to win permission from Luisa's father. Colonel Arismendi was in competition with many suitors, most much younger. But Luisa had been immediately drawn to the colonel from the moment she was introduced, and she desperately wanted her father to approve of the union. Despite the wishes of his daughter and Colonel Arismendi, Luisa's father did not grant his blessing.

The following year, her father was killed after being set up by Royalist forces looking to capture anyone close to patriot forces. Her father was friendly with many officers in the patriot forces, but he assiduously avoided open talk of rebellion and took pained steps to remain as neutral as possible. Royalist forces noticed his friendship with another colonel and friend of Arismendi. Mr. Cáceres traveled to visit the commandant of the coastal town of Ocumare, a close friend of Cáceres, when it was invaded by Royalist troops. Upon hearing of the peril Luisa's father and the others were in, Colonel Arismendi led a failed attempt to rescue the imprisoned patriots. Luisa's brother was killed during the ensuing battle. Patriot forces were subsequently pushed out of Caracas. In exodus, the remainder of Luisa's family fled to the protection afforded on Isla Margarita by Colonel Arismendi, who took them and cared for them, providing food, shelter, and all else they would need to live. It seemed that the fates had brought Colonel Arismendi and Luisa Cáceres together. The shared hardships and fight for survival against the Royalists had cemented their relationship, and they were soon married.

While General Arismendi was fighting Royalist forces, including hardened troops of the Napoleonic Wars, Luisa was held captive in a dungeon with little food or water. To force his surrender, General Moxo had ordered the arrest of Luisa. She was routinely subjected to torture, including numerous fake executions. She would be placed before a firing squad and offered a reprieve if she renounced the support of the patriot cause and assisted in the apprehension of her husband. She repeatedly remained loyal to her husband and country, choosing the firing squad instead. The firing squads would shoot their rifles, but she would not be hit. This was repeated multiple times. Her brave stance against her captors was reported by the women who tended to her inside the fortress during the captivity and led to the spread of news of her heroism. The depredations likely caused the miscarriage of her baby while she was held in the dungeon. General Moxo wrote to General Morillo how satisfied he was that the little Arismendi monster had died and pushed for the actual execution of Luisa.

The treatment of his wife only served to make General Arismendi fight even harder. He continued as a leader of the patriot troops and persisted in insurrections against the Spanish forces.

After more than a year in captivity, Luisa was removed from the island before the last remaining Spanish strongpoints fell to the onslaught of General Arismendi's forces. General Moxo provided instructions to Captain Naves of the vessel *El Populo* that would transport Luisa back to Spain. In those instructions, he stated that she would be arraigned in Cadiz as a prisoner of war and would be brought before the king so that she could account for her actions and those of her tyrant husband. Two Spanish warships would escort the *El Populo*.

The flotilla departed from La Guaira, Venezuela, in November 1816. During the journey, the three-ship contingent was pursued by several pirate ships determined to capture the Spanish vessels. In an interesting twist, the passengers on board the vessel and the captain himself believed that General Arismendi led the ships pursuing them. They begged Luisa to intercede on their behalf to spare their lives. She felt it was nearly impossible that General Arismendi knew she had boarded a ship bound for Spain, that it could not possibly be him or those that he had sent. But to ease the fears of the others on board, although she was just a girl and a prisoner of King Ferdinand being sent possibly to her death, she assured them that they would all be spared—she would make sure of it.

The pirates closed, firing cannons, rifles, and pistols. They quickly boarded the ships and captured them one by one. Fighting with swords and pistols was taking place all around her. In short order, the crew and passengers surrendered to the pirates. Their leader, an American with a letter of marque that authorized him to privateer, informed everyone that they were his hostages.

When the American learned that Luisa was a prisoner of the Spanish Crown, he offered her freedom. She was overwhelmed but determined to face her destiny before the king. She declined the offer of freedom and pledged to cooperate with the Spanish captain. The hostages were dropped off at the Azores, a set of Portuguese islands in the middle of the Atlantic Ocean. The group purchased a run-down ship, refitted it, and continued on their journey to Cadiz. Her fellow passengers and even the ship's captain treated her very differently after witnessing the bravery she displayed before the pirates. She had eased their fears when they thought they faced certain death, and when offered her liberty, she chose instead to follow the directive of the Crown. The group finally arrived in Cadiz, Spain, in January 1817.

Luisa was sent to a prison in Spain, where her mistreatment continued, yet she held fast to the love of her country, Venezuela, to the ideals of liberty, and to her husband. She was brought before the king and told to bow before him, renounce her political views, and sign a loyalty oath.

She refused, reportedly telling him, "With all due respect, I will not. You are not my king."

The fact that the young woman was educated and well mannered as she curtsied before the king before defying him greatly impressed an English diplomat who was at court. The Englishman would later have a hand in helping her escape.

The governor of the Andalusian region of Spain, an area that operated with some degree of autonomy, was sympathetic to Luisa's plight. The governor allowed her to be merely "confined" and held under the patronage of a prominent couple, who agreed to take her in and see to it that she reported regularly to a local judge. But thanks to a Spanish lieutenant and the aforementioned Englishman, who befriended her and agreed to help her, she was smuggled onto the *Ruth and Mary*, a merchant ship anchored in Cadiz but bound for Philadelphia. She climbed on board with a single trunk and her bedding, arriving on May 2, 1818.

In Philadelphia, she lived with an American couple and quickly became a celebrity among the city's elite. Eventually, General Juan Bautista Arismendi was able to dispatch a colonel to bring her back to Venezuela, where she was reunited with her husband at Isla Margarita in July 1818. The couple eventually had eleven children, and due to her unflagging support for the principles of freedom and self-determination, she became a true heroine of the South American struggle for independence.

Luisa Cáceres de Arismendi died in 1866 and became the first woman to be buried in the Panteón Nacional, a memorial to Venezuela's heroes in Caracas. There is a statue of her in the plaza, which also bears her name in the small village where she was married. A college in the capital is named after her, and her likeness is featured on the current twenty bolívar fuerte banknote.

At the Santa Rosa Fortress, where she was first imprisoned, a plaque commemorating her reads, "Luisa Cáceres de Arismendi for her virtue, valor, and martyrdom for husband and country. Held captive in this jail."

Acknowledgments

THIS BOOK HAS BEEN A LIFETIME IN THE MAKING; MANY PEOPLE have contributed to this work directly or indirectly. I would like to express my sincere gratitude and appreciation to a number of them. First and foremost, I want to thank the Creator, that unseen intelligence and power in the universe that goes by many names.

To my family and friends, past and present, words cannot express my gratitude. Thank you for all the love and memories.

To my mom, Cecilia Pardi de Ramia, thank you for teaching me to believe in myself, to survive and thrive against all odds, to be relentlessly driven, and to never take shit from anyone.

To Helen Arismendi, my American mom, thank you for always treating me like a son, for your generosity, love, kindness, and support.

To my dad, the Reverend Edward Arismendi, thank you for all your love, encouragement, guidance, and inspiration.

To my brother, Dr. Eduardo Jesús Arismendi-Pardi, thank you for always having my back since we were kids. You were always there to help me and were by my side ready to fight.

To my sister, Angela María Arismendi-Pardi, you were my best friend growing up, so many great memories.

To my little sister, Maria de Los Angeles Wong-Arismendi-Pardi, you brighten every room with your presence.

To my ex-wife, Alyssa Arismendi, an amazing mom to both our sons, I'm grateful for our time together.

To my amazing sons, Anthony and Dillon, two beautiful, kind, and loving souls, I'm grateful you chose me as your dad.

To my friend Larry Cano, thank you for helping to bring my stories to life. You are a truly talented writer with an uncanny ability to feel and see the nuances of every moment.

To Christine Christensen, my love and inspiration, thank you for your never-ending encouragement, support, and help in making this book a reality. I love you.

To my best friend Rich Kincaid, without a doubt one of the best FBI agents I have ever worked with, a true warrior and most loyal friend, I thank you for always having my back.

To my best friend Jim Lacey for taking me under your wing from day one, as a newly minted FBI agent, and always being in my corner.

To the amazing team at Scribe Media for overdelivering! Starting with Aleza D'Agostino, my project manager; Esty Pittman, my publishing manager; Charity Young, my first editor; Chip Blake, my second editor; Erin Sky, my copywriter; Skyler Gray, my genius title expert; Michael Nagin, a true master cover designer—simply amazing! And the marketing and design team.

Finally, to all the outsiders, the ones who risk it all and go against the grain. The ones who never play it safe, live on the edge, and are not afraid to be themselves. I thank you all, for you make our world a better place.

About the Author

ANTHONY ARISMENDI IS A FORMER FBI AGENT WITH A HIGHLY decorated and distinguished career spanning two decades of undercover operations against drug cartels, gangs, organized crime, violent criminals, and terrorist organizations. He has served as a member of the FBI's SWAT team, as a supervisory agent in two field offices and FBI Headquarters, and as a unit chief in the FBI's Criminal Investigative Division. He is the recipient of the Hispanic American Police Command Officer's Association's (HAPCOA) Medal of Meritorious Service, the Special Act Award from the Drug Enforcement Administration (DEA), the Internal Revenue Service (IRS) Commissioner's Criminal Investigator's Award, and he was recognized by FBI Director Louis J. Freeh for his nomination to the prestigious FBI Director's Award for Excellence in Investigations.

Today, he is the President and CEO of ARIXMAR and a sought-after public speaker, sharing his compelling and motivating story with public and private organizations across the country.

Larry Cano is an entrepreneur, writer, and UCLA graduate film school alum best known for his role as executive producer of the Oscar-nominated movie *Silkwood* starring Meryl Streep, Cher, and Kurt Russell.

Made in the USA
Las Vegas, NV
12 January 2023

65484745R00173